W9-CMT-304

Landmark
BOOKS

Evangeline and the Acadians

Other Landmark Books by Robert Tallant

THE PIRATE LAFITTE & THE BATTLE OF NEW ORLEANS

THE LOUISIANA PURCHASE

EVANGELINE AND THE ACADIANS

by **ROBERT TALLANT**

Illustrated by **CORINNE BOYD DILLON**

RANDOM HOUSE : NEW YORK

Third Printing

 Published in New York by Random House, Inc., and simultaneously in Toronto, Canada, by Random House of Canada, Limited.

Library of Congress Catalog Card Number: 54-6264

Manufactured in the United States of America

Contents

Evangeline and the Acadians

1 *The First Frenchmen*

IN THAT PART OF CANADA WE NOW CALL NOVA SCOTIA A Frenchman with the long name of Timothé Pierre du Gast, Sieur de Monts, will always be famous. He is mentioned in American history, too, but seldom has enough been told about him. Yet the inscription on his statue in the Nova Scotian town of Annapolis calls him the pioneer of civilization in North America and describes him as the founder of the first European settlement north of the Gulf of Mexico. It is certainly true that in 1604 he did found the first permanent French colony on this continent. This was three years before the founding of Jamestown in Virginia and sixteen years before the *Mayflower* brought the Pilgrims to Plymouth Rock.

Of course other Frenchmen had come to the New World a long time before. Fishermen living along the northwest coast of France had heard of the fine fishing around Newfoundland and the rocky shores of New England and some had attempted voyages to these regions. In 1506 one of them, John Denys, reached the Gulf of St. Lawrence. He drew a crude map of this part of America, and this, together with the tales he told, drew others toward the New World.

Later, in 1524, the king of France sent an Italian navigator named Verrazano to America. He explored the coast of America from what is now North Carolina to the northern part of New England.

Exactly ten years later, Jacques Cartier entered the Gulf of St. Lawrence. In 1535 he claimed the country for the French king, and traveled as far west as the present city of Montreal. Six years later Cartier built a fort on the site of Quebec.

But these and other attempted French settlements in the sixteenth century were failures. Trouble with the Indians, the cold winters and the lack of food brought disaster and death to the French settlers.

Then in 1604 De Monts, a nobleman in the court of Henry IV of France, arrived in the New World. His king promised him a grant of the rights to all the fur trading in the region if he could successfully establish a colony. With De Monts were three other Frenchmen,

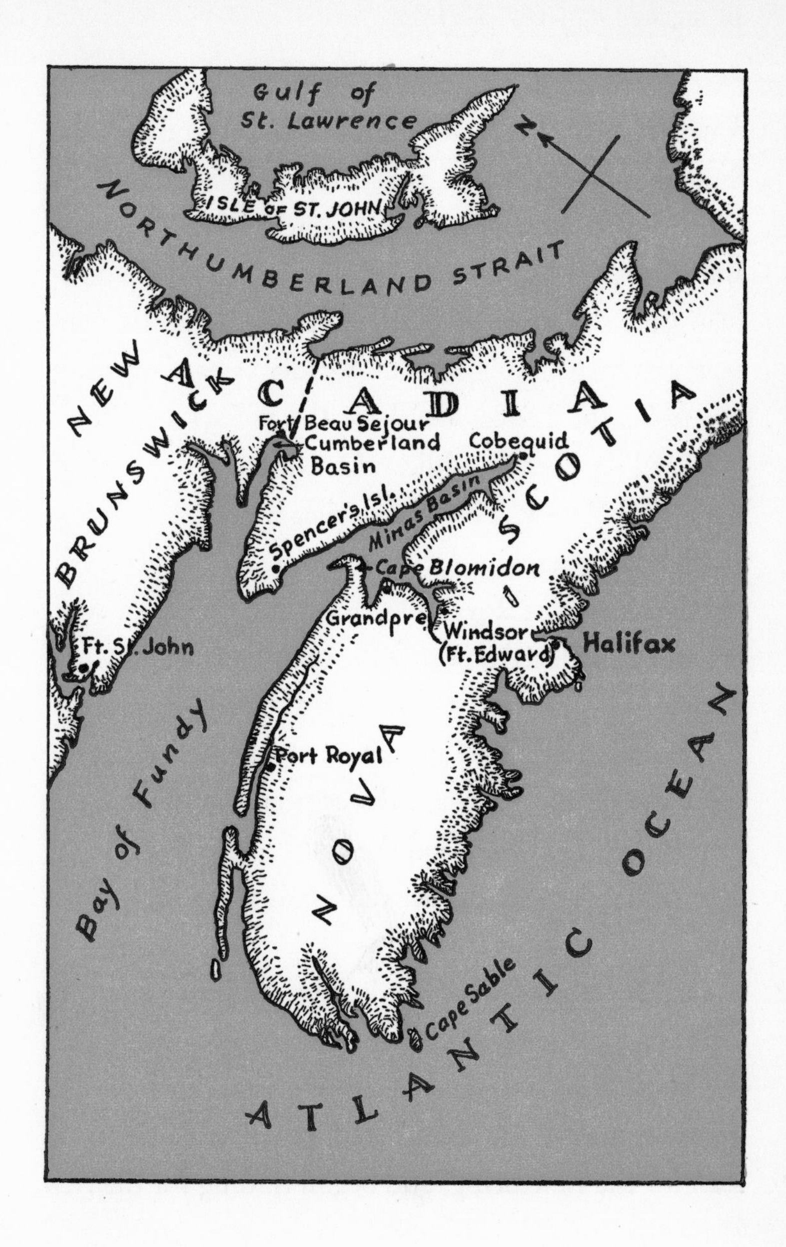

Gulf of
St. Lawrence
N
ISLE OF ST. JOHN
NORTHUMBERLAND STRAIT
NEW BRUNSWICK
ACADIA
NOVA SCOTIA
Fort Beau Sejour
Cumberland
Basin
Cobequid
Spencer's Isl.
Minas Basin
Cape Blomidon
Grandpre
Windsor
(Ft. Edward)
Halifax
Ft. St. John
Bay of Fundy
Port Royal
Cape Sable
ATLANTIC OCEAN

two of whom were named Pontgrave and Poutrincourt. The third man was destined to become the most famous member of the party, for he was Samuel de Champlain, often called the "Father of New France." But it was De Monts who led the party, and it was he who gave the name of Acadie, or Acadia, to the land now known as Nova Scotia. "Acadia" was taken from *aquoddie,* the Indian word for the pollack, a fish.

Joined by French soldiers, De Monts' party entered the Bay of Fundy. This harbor pleased Poutrincourt so much that he remained there with a few followers, calling the place Port Royal. De Monts and the others went on, and established a post at the mouth of the St. Croix River.

Then the terrible winter set in. By spring half of the party was dead of scurvy, a disease that results from improper diet. De Monts led the rest back to Port Royal. The history of Acadia, as well as all Canada, had begun.

De Monts was a strong, honest, and able man, as well as a patriotic Frenchman. He got along well with the Micmacs—Indians who were a branch of the Algonquin tribes. He established peace with them, at least for the time being, and began trading for the rich

De Monts traded with the Micmacs for rich furs

furs he wanted to ship back to France. Champlain went on to explore the country, to found Quebec, and to travel south and discover what is now Lake Champlain. But De Monts remained in his Acadia.

In 1613 the English raided Port Royal and burned the tiny village. Hard times followed, but the French settlers remained in Acadia. There was another invasion of Acadia in 1621. The English tried to settle there, calling the place Nova Scotia, or New Scotland. This was the start of the long wars between France and England for territory in the New World, but the Frenchmen at Port Royal stood their ground.

In 1628 the English captured Port Royal once more, but in 1632 France regained all Acadia. Back and forth the fighting went. First one side would win, and then the other. In 1667, Acadia was once more in the hands of the French.

At that time there were only about four hundred persons living at Port Royal and a scattering of others living near by. These were the people who were coming to be known as Acadians. Most of them had come from the northwest provinces of France, and almost all were simple but hardy peasants, fisher-folk and farmers.

As early as 1636 the Acadians had begun to build dikes to hold back the salt tides that always threatened the marshlands of the region. About 1670 they began to push northward and to develop the country near Grandpré, which means Great Prairie. This was to become their principal settlement. It was of these Acadians of Grandpré that Longfellow wrote in his famous poem, *Evangeline*.

The Acadians had many children and during the next twenty years the population increased to more than double its former size. Then, in 1689, France and England went to war again, and the English invaded and captured the fertile valleys of the Acadians.

This was a horrible war, and fighting raged for years. Both the French and the English used Indians in savage attacks upon each other. The Acadians themselves took almost no part in this struggle, but tried their best to live in peace on the farms they had built. They were French and their loyalty was to France, but they had come to the New World to build homes and a future for their children. As a result, they tried to remain outside of the quarrels of the government at home in France.

Port Royal fell to the British for the last time in 1710,

when a garrison of less than three hundred men surrendered to forces from New England. At that hour Acadia was lost to France forever. Its name was changed to Nova Scotia, and that of Port Royal to Annapolis, in honor of Queen Anne of England. The Baie Française became the Bay of Fundy, and almost all other names in the section were changed. Yet Grandpré, the Acadians' principal home, retained that name, which it still does today, long, long after the Acadians have been gone.

In 1713, by the Treaty of Utrecht, Louis XIV of France surrendered to England all rights to Acadia or Nova Scotia. After the English soldiers took charge at Annapolis and other towns in the vicinity, some English settlers came. Only a few of these settled near Grandpré.

Whatever their feelings as Frenchmen, the Acadians tried to get along with the newcomers. They must have hoped that peace would be permanent and that they could go on cultivating their fields. They wanted no more of the noise of war and the sight of blood.

The Treaty of Utrecht had granted them certain rights. They were to be allowed to practice their own religion, for they were Catholic while the English were Protestant. They were also given the right to move to other Canadian provinces, which remained French, and to take with them all of their belongings that they could carry.

Few Acadians did this. Their homes were built, and their farms were flourishing. Even though they disliked English rule, they did not want to give all this up. Why should they start all over again in new territory? Why should they once more go through the labor and agony of breaking ground and rock, of building new homes and starting new fields and pastures? So they remained.

They kept their religion, their customs and their language. They continued to be as French as they had ever been, even though living on soil that was now British.

For a long time the British did not consider the Acadians large enough in number to become troublesome or dangerous. In 1713 the English counted only some three hundred families of Acadians. They do not seem to have been bothered then by the fact that many Acadian families had from twelve to twenty children!

Queen Anne of England died in 1714, and George I

came to the throne. The next year Lieutenant Governor Caulfield of Nova Scotia thought that the Acadians should now swear to be subjects of the new English king and, in case of war, should fight with the British.

The Acadians refused to take the oath, and no attempts were made to force them to do so at that time. Each year after that they were again asked to pledge their allegiance to England, and for eleven years they refused. Finally, in 1726, the Acadians took the oath—but only in part. In return they were granted the right to remain neutral in any future war, for they refused to bear arms against the French, the Indians, or any other nation or race, including the English themselves.

This oath, accepted by officers of the British army at Grandpré, was not considered satisfactory by the new governor of Nova Scotia. Four years later, in 1730, the Acadians took another oath, and this time without written conditions. However, they always insisted that they had the governor's promise in words, although not in writing, that they would never be asked to fight against other Frenchmen or against the Indians.

Whatever the truth of this, the Acadians were let alone for more than twenty years. During that period they enjoyed the peace they wanted, although there was much discontent among them over British rule. Meanwhile their numbers increased. It is believed that by 1750 there were sixteen thousand Acadians living at Grandpré!

2 *This Was Grandpré*

ACADIA WAS NOT QUITE AS IT IS DESCRIBED BY LONGfellow in *Evangeline,* but it was a beautiful land. Across the peninsula stretched the Cobequid, a mountain range whose blue summits loomed against the sky.

The winters were severe, it is true, with temperatures that often dropped to twenty below zero, but in the coldest weather the Acadians were comfortable. Their houses were stout and well made, with thick walls and thatched roofs. Their barns were sturdy and provided storage for grain and other food. There was always hope, too, for the winters ended in lovely springs and summers. Then the rich earth returned to life with plentiful crops and brilliant flowers.

The slopes and valleys of Grandpré were well watered and extremely fertile. Cool mountain streams ran through the land and the deep wells were filled with icy water.

In this rich land, the Acadians raised wheat and other grains, flax, and a huge variety of vegetables. Apple orchards flourished. The peaches did not do so well, but there were pears and plums. Potatoes thrived. The cattle of the Acadians were fat, and their yards were filled with chickens and geese, and clipped wild turkeys. There were pigs for roasting whole, and for lard, bacon and fine hams.

The life of the Acadians was simple by our standards, and every man and woman worked hard, but it was a good life. They rarely saw money, but almost every family owned its own home, its own barnyard, and raised most of its own food. What a man lacked he would get from his neighbor by bartering. A young man who was newly married would be helped by all his relatives and neighbors to build his own cottage. Wedding gifts would include young pigs, a calf or two, chickens, and seed, so that the couple could start life with the beginnings of their farm.

The typical Acadian cottage was built of logs. All chinks and crevices were sealed with clay and earth. Roofs were thatched, and usually a trap door led down into a stone cellar for the storing of potatoes and dried apples.

Most of the cottages were taken up by a huge center room in which there was a very large stone fireplace which provided heat. It was big enough for the roasting of a side of calf or a whole pig, and in it cooking pots were hung. In this center room the mother and the father and perhaps the youngest children might sleep. Older children had sleeping quarters in a loft reached from the main room by a ladder.

The Acadians—men, women and children—kept busy, for there was much work to be done. The men hunted and trapped and fished. Together with the women, they also worked in the fields. When a boy was old enough he joined his father in the farm work and went hunting with him. Girls helped their mothers in the housekeeping chores. There were candles to be made, cheeses to be tended, geese to be plucked, cloth to be spun. Because the Acadians made all their own cloth for clothing and for household use, the spinning wheel had a place of importance by the fire.

There were quilts as well as linens and fine lace to be made. Many families made their own shoes, tanning the leather and sewing it with stout thread also made at home. The village of Grandpré boasted a bootmaker and a blacksmith, but the Acadian family made most of its own belongings. Among the articles of home manufacture were pots and other cooking vessels, clay or pewter bowls and dishes, and knives and forks.

Mattresses and pillows were homemade, too, stuffed with goose feathers or soft, fragrant pine needles. Grain was ground into flour, then baked into bread. A family made all its own jellies and preserves and wine—in fact, almost everything it ate and drank and used.

But life was not all work. The Acadians were a gay people, who loved laughter and fun. There were village musicians and village dances. Everybody knew everybody else, and there were many celebrations—weddings, christenings, parties of all kinds. They were an affectionate people, close to each other, fond of their own kind.

Yet they got on well with other people too—with everyone, that is, but the English. They had almost no trouble with the Micmac Indians. They mixed with them freely and a few intermarried with them, so that some Acadian families had a strain of Indian blood. Their priests converted many Micmacs to the Christian faith.

The priests were important at Grandpré. The church there, which will play an important part in this story, was the center of the life of the village. It was to a priest that the Acadian went with all his troubles. It was a priest who gave all help in any legal matters, and who was the adviser at all times.

The Acadians were not educated in reading and writing. There were no schools. Travelers among them wrote home that it was not known if any Acadian could even sign his name. Boys and girls learned all the work and the skills necessary to the way of life of their people, but they received no book learning. They used their hands for everything but writing, their eyes for everything but reading. Education as we know it would have been of little if any use to them. In the oath of allegiance they finally signed with the English, all signed their names with a cross.

Their village and their homes may have been crude, but they were pretty. The Acadians loved flowers and almost every family had a garden of tall lilacs and vivid roses; vines trailed to the thatched roofs. The people themselves were a handsome race—the men stocky and strong, the women striking, with brilliant black eyes and hair, white teeth, and fine features.

They were also very clean. An Acadian housewife prided herself upon her scrubbed and gleaming floors, her shining cooking utensils, and her white linens. Barns and outbuildings were kept as orderly and neat as the cottages. Cattle and fowl were healthy and sleek.

Of course life was far from perfect at Grandpré or in the rest of Acadia, even before the English came. The Acadians had more than their share of trouble. They had come to wild and primitive country as had all European settlers in the New World. The farms and fields had to be made from the raw and unconquered earth. Nature had to be fought constantly.

Large tracts of their country was marshland, most of it lying north of Grandpré. Dikes had to be built to keep out the sea. When the sea rolled in, as it sometimes did, a year's crop might be ruined. The bitter winters brought illness and death to many of the earliest of these settlers. Later, as they grew in numbers and learned how to make their houses stronger and how to live in the climate, they were better able to adjust themselves to the bitter winters.

The "primeval forest" described by Longfellow was farther away than he described it, but it provided the Acadians with wood for heat and for cooking. During the summer they stored wood for winter use.

Although their lives were usually peaceful, the Aca-

On winter evenings they gathered about the huge fire

dians quarreled among themselves at times, especially in the years before the English came. Quarrels came over boundary lines between farms and fields, between families. Yet, as a whole, they seem to have got along fairly well with one another. And against outsiders they seem to have stood together as one.

Most of the time they were too busy for quarreling. Chore followed chore. The hay must be got in, the wheat cut, the cattle and fowl fed. There was milking to be done, there were eggs to be gathered. On Saturdays they might wander in the village, trading their produce, gossiping, the children playing, the young men waiting to meet their girls at a Saturday night dance. Sunday was devoted to church and visiting, and long walks in the lovely apple orchards.

In the cold winter evenings the Acadian families would gather about the huge fire in the main room of their homes. The women would run their spinning wheels, sew, or crochet. The children would sit on the floor at the hearth with their pet cats or dogs. The men would smoke and talk, sometimes working the while at a new fishing net or cleaning a gun.

Like most simple people, they were fond of stories, and often an older man or woman would spend the evening telling long tales. Some of these had been handed down from parents or grandparents who had brought them from France. Very often the stories were about the kings and princes and knights of the homeland across the sea. Sometimes they were about goblins and witches and the werewolves that were called *loups-garous*.

Other stories the Acadians had learned from the Indians. The Micmacs had many of their own legends and fairy tales. A favorite story was of Glooscap, the Great Spirit of the Micmac tribe.

Once, it was said, Glooscap had lived in Acadia or Nova Scotia. It was his home, his land. He had a huge wigwam on Cape Blomidon. All the places in Nova Scotia had been his possessions. Minas Basin was his beaver pond. Spencer's Island was his kettle. Two huge rocks near by were his dogs. Then the white man came. Glooscap thought the white man treacherous. He turned over his kettle, changed his dogs to rocks, and vanished. He would come back one day, the Micmacs said, after the white man left. They did not know where he had gone, but they were waiting for his return.

When all the stories were told, the evening would end. And it would end early, for there was much to be done the next morning. Candles in their hands, the boys and girls would climb up into their lofts, and the parents would go to bed in the great room below.

Thus did the Acadians live. Life was hard as far as work went, but even some of their work brought them joy. They especially enjoyed hunting for wild game, fishing in boats, and trapping the beaver. All these skills were taught to the young boys as soon as they were old enough. At reaping time the women and girls sang in the fields. Their apple orchards gave them joy, as did all their living possessions—their oxen and cattle, their fat geese, their pets. In all but money they were rich.

Life was secure and happy. There was much food. If a man was willing to work he was not likely to suffer for want of any of the necessities of life.

It must have seemed to the Acadians that nothing would ever change. They must have felt they had established and built a world of their own that would go on forever.

Then the English came in larger numbers.

3 *The Arrival of the English*

ACADIA HAD BELONGED TO ENGLAND SINCE 1713. IN 1730 the French residents had taken their oath of allegiance to the British crown. And for more than twenty years after that there was peace between the two peoples. There was dislike and fear on both sides, but there was little open disturbance.

For one thing, the English living near the Acadians were few in number. There was almost no mixing between the two nationalities. The Acadians continued speaking their own language and practicing their own religion. They called the country Acadia still, while the English called it Nova Scotia. The Acadians ignored the English soldiers and government as much as possible. They were closer to the Micmacs than to these newcomers.

But the English knew they were the rulers and their anger against the Acadians grew. There were many causes for this. For one thing, the English simply did not like the Acadians, who behaved as if they owned the country. Secondly, the English resented the very simplicity of the Acadians, and what they considered their ignorance. Also, the English were jealous of how well the Acadians managed to live in this primitive country.

Then, too, the English feared the Micmacs, who were not as friendly with them as they were with the Acadians. Gradually the English began to fear that the Acadians would fight on the side of the Indians in case of war. They knew the Acadians felt no loyalty at all toward England.

Finally, and most important, England and France during this period were struggling for control of America. Since the Acadians were French, the English feared they would help the French of Canada against the English in any war between the two nations. They did not feel secure as long as the Acadians remained French and did not become British subjects.

This smoldered for a long time. More English came to Nova Scotia; more soldiers were sent to the forts and villages. Yet the Acadians grew more numerous too. Every year they seemed more and more dangerous to the English. Whispered rumors became widespread. The English told one another that the Acadians and Indians were planning to wipe them out.

It is unlikely that the Acadians had any such plans. They were a quiet people who did not want war. Acadian boys might jeer at passing British soldiers, Acadian men might make sly remarks in which were mingled dislike and humor, but all they really wanted was freedom to live their own way. Certainly they would never have helped the British against the Micmacs. But neither would they have aided the Indians against the British. They wanted to be neutral. Or so they always maintained.

Then, a bit later, things seem to have changed a little. When war broke out again between France and England, many Acadians left Nova Scotia for French territory, and these men did take arms against Great Britain. In addition, the British charged that many Acadians who remained at home had secret meetings with French troops, furnished French soldiers with supplies, and acted as French spies. They were even accused of giving arms and ammunition to the Indians who attacked the British.

Whether or not all or part of this was true may always be a mystery. Historians have argued about it for years. Descendants of the Acadians have always denied it. English and some American writers have believed the Acadians were guilty. Probably no one knows.

Peace between England and France came again in 1748, with the signing of the Peace Treaty of Aix-la-Chapelle. Under this agreement Nova Scotia again became English territory.

Now both the Acadians and the English were more bitter than ever. More Acadians left for the French part of Canada. Some of those who remained were angry because they thought that their Acadia should have been given back to France. On the other hand, the English felt they could never trust the Acadians again. They suspected even the priests of being spies.

Meanwhile, another source of irritation had developed. In 1743 an advertisement in the *London Gazette* had brought a large number of English settlers to Nova Scotia. This was the beginning of the town of Halifax. By 1748 this settlement contained more than 4,000 English people.

Neither the Acadians nor the Micmacs were pleased by this. The French in that part of Canada belonging to France sent messages by Indian scouts encouraging the bad feeling of the Acadians. The Micmacs made raids on Halifax, and during one raid took eighteen English scalps.

According to Francis Parkman, the great American historian, Acadian men sometimes disguised themselves as Indians and took part in these raids. Whether this was true or not, it was what the English believed. They blamed the Acadians for all their trouble with the Micmac tribe.

The new governor, Cornwallis, demanded in 1749 that the Acadians take a new oath of loyalty to England or be severely punished. Under this oath they would be called upon to help the British fight the Indians and any other enemies, which would include the other Canadian French, should war break out again. Everyone knew war between France and England was likely to start again at any time. Then the Acadians would find themselves fighting their brothers. Once more they refused to take the oath.

This demand seemed to the Acadians an act of tyranny, and it has seemed so to many people since. Yet the British felt they had no choice. They argued that no group of people living in their territory could

The Acadians asked permission to leave Nova Scotia

remain neutral and still be trusted. To them that was all that mattered.

At about this time representatives of Acadians appeared before Governor Cornwallis and asked permission to leave Nova Scotia forever. (This was the uncle of the Cornwallis who was defeated at Yorktown, years later, in the American War of Independence.) With them, the Acadians said they would take only what they could carry—their clothes and some household goods. They wanted to go to the provinces of Canada that were still French.

This Cornwallis forbade. He knew that if he allowed the Acadians to join the other French settlers across the border, he would be giving the French hundreds of additional soldiers to fight against the English. He told them they must remain.

The Acadians were now in a strange position. They were not wanted, yet they were forbidden to leave. They could not swear to fight with the English against their own people, yet they could not join their own people. They felt the homes they had made and loved were no longer really theirs. Yet they must remain in them. In a way they had become prisoners in these homes.

Time went on and nothing much happened. Cornwallis did ask them several more times to take the oath, which they would not do. Some of the more adventurous Acadians escaped across the border into French territory. Cornwallis departed, and another governor came, this time a man named Hopson. He, too, tried to get the Acadians to pledge loyalty to Great Britain, as usual without success.

Naturally such a state of affairs could not last. The Acadians came to look upon the English as their guards in a prison. The English considered the Acadians dangerous fanatics, enemies, a sinister foe who waited only for an opportunity to do them harm, if possible to drive them from Nova Scotia and take back the country for their own. This the Acadians would certainly have done if they could, but for all their numbers, and even with the help of the Micmacs, they did not have the power to do so. All they could do was to stand firm and refuse to be English.

Then, in 1754, Charles Lawrence came to take Hopson's place as Governor of Nova Scotia.

4 *Governor Lawrence's Decision*

CHARLES LAWRENCE HAD BEEN A MAJOR IN THE BRITISH infantry, a chancellor in Governor Cornwallis' cabinet, and finally the lieutenant-governor of Nova Scotia. He was a stern man with an irritable disposition and no friend of the Acadians. He saw them only as a threat to British power.

When he became governor, Lawrence was determined that the situation between the British and the Acadians would not go on as it had for so many years. He was bitter against the French priests and especially against one, Father Le Loutre, whom the Acadians followed as a leader.

More than anything else, Lawrence feared that Le Loutre would persuade all the Acadians to escape to French Canada where they would take up arms against the British.

Yet even Lawrence seems to have been inclined to be patient when he first took office. In 1754 he wrote to the English Board of Trade as follows: "I believe that a very large part of the Acadians would submit to any terms rather than take up arms on either side." This was proof that he then believed the Acadians could be talked into remaining neutral when war broke out again.

But Lawrence did not have very much patience, and during the next few months what little he had wore thin. More and more reports reached him of Acadians slipping across the border, of their acting as spies, and of the meetings of Father Le Loutre with the Micmacs.

Too, Lawrence was much worried about the growing military preparations of the French. One fort, called Beau Séjour, bothered him more than anything else. It had been erected by the French in 1749 on the side of the isthmus that was in New Brunswick, next door to Nova Scotia and just beyond the border between French and British territories.

There had long been misunderstanding between both nations as to the boundaries of Acadia or Nova Scotia, and the British claimed that New Brunswick (and even a portion beyond) was theirs. Yet the French flag waved triumphantly above Beau Séjour and it was occupied by French soldiers and by Acadians. It was a situation Lawrence could not tolerate.

Late in the spring of 1755, after corresponding with each other for several months, Lawrence and Governor William Shirley of Massachusetts decided that Beau Séjour must go. They sent a force of about two thousand militia troops to take it. In June Beau Séjour fell to the British.

In connection with the expedition against Beau Séjour, Governor Lawrence had written to General Braddock, who was then in charge of the military operations against the French, as follows:

> *I esteem it my duty to acquaint you that, in case of a rupture with France, my forces will in no ways be in proportion to the number of posts which we must be obliged to defend, especially if it be considered that, even in the heart of the province, we have what we call neutral French (Acadians), inhabitants well armed and connected with the French king; so that upon the least attempt which Canada would make to invade us, I believe it is more than probable that they would immediately join them (the other French in Canada).*

The victory at Beau Séjour pleased Lawrence, but he was far from satisfied. He decided upon drastic means to get rid of the Acadians. He decided they must be exiled from Nova Scotia forever!

This was the beginning of the end.

Now Governor Lawrence summoned a group of Acadian deputies. He ordered these men to swear an oath of allegiance to King George II. If they refused they were to be declared rebels and could be shot. To protect their lives the men took the oath.

Next Lawrence sent orders to Captain Handfield, the British officer at old Port Royal, now called Annapolis, and to Captain Alexander Murray at Windsor. Handfield and Murray were to inform the Acadians living in those places that they were to be cast out of their homeland and must prepare themselves for departure.

Colonel Moncton, now in charge at Beau Séjour, was commanded to seize all able-bodied Acadians near by and hold them for further orders. Colonel Winslow of Massachusetts was ordered to march to Grandpré. The settlements at Minas, Cobequid and Rivière aux Canards were also ordered invaded by British troops.

The poor Acadians! We must remember that they were very simple people. They were uneducated, at least in the kind of learning we get from schools and books. Perhaps they were guilty of doing harm to the British, but at least in their own minds they felt they were right.

For one thing, they had been the first white people to make their homes in Nova Scotia, or at least their ancestors had been. Most of them had never known any other home.

And their homes had been made with their own hands. The cottages and cabins had been built with their own hard labor, the land cultivated. They were industrious, frugal. They had made their lives secure by years of toil and suffering. Many of their grandparents and their great-grandparents had died trying to carve a homeland out of the wilderness, the prairies, the salt marshes. Nova Scotia was their country in every sense of the word except that it had been conquered by the English.

The resentment they felt against the English was natural. The English were invaders so far as they were concerned. This was how the Indians felt, too. It was why the Micmacs and the Acadians had always stood together. The Acadians had never taken anything away from the Indians. They had asked only that they be allowed to live side by side with the Indians. They had treated them as equals. They had mixed with them. There was enough land for everyone, and the Micmacs had cared little that the Acadians used part of it. The Acadians had not come as conquerors.

The English had always been different. They wanted to found a colony in Nova Scotia too, but they wanted it all to themselves. Besides, they did not look upon either the Acadians or the Micmacs as friends and equals. So it was natural also that both the Acadians and the Micmacs felt drawn together against them.

Now it was all over. The English knew they could get rid of the Indians. They could chase them out, drive them farther into the wilderness, shoot them. But first the Acadians had to go. They must be dealt with in a different way, but they had to be removed. Then Nova Scotia would become a completely English colony. There was no place in it, Governor Lawrence had decided, for a group of people so dangerous to English interests as the Acadians.

5 *Prisoners of the King!*

LAWRENCE HAD DECIDED THAT THE ACADIANS MUST BE exiled. The question now was where to send them. Messages were sent to London, asking for an answer to the problem. The long summer months of 1755 passed while the Governor and the other British authorities, and the Acadians themselves, awaited a reply.

Probably most of the Acadians hoped that in the end they would be allowed to remain in their homes. Certainly none of them could have realized what lay ahead.

Meanwhile, the British were making plans—cold, hard, and ruthless plans. Colonel Winslow and Captain Murray met in Windsor at the new Fort Edward. Acting under orders from Governor Lawrence, they drew up a paper on how to deal with the problem at Grandpré.

No message approving this paper ever came from George II, but it was carried out none the less. Every

Acadian male aged ten and over in the area around Grandpré was to appear at the village church on the fifth of September to hear the reading of a paper approved by the Governor and His Majesty, the King. This was Lawrence's lie. He had heard nothing from the King.

Autumn comes early in Nova Scotia, but that September fifth must have seemed the coldest any Acadian could recall. The fall coloring of the leaves must have seemed faded and the bright, wild skies less splendid as the males, young and old, rode or trudged on foot toward the church. Until then their church had been a refuge, a haven of peace. Suddenly it must have seemed a place filled with terror.

We are told four hundred eighteen men and boys stood together in the tiny Church of St. Charles at Grandpré. The scene there was repeated at Annapolis, at Minas, at Windsor, and in every other part of Acadia. We know more about Grandpré because of the poem of *Evangeline,* telling her tragic story, but it was the same wherever Acadians lived.

Colonel Winslow spoke in the Church of St. Charles, standing in the pulpit where Father Le Loutre had once stood. Winslow was a fat man with a round red

Colonel Winslow told them they were to be exiled

face. In his portraits he looks cheerful and full of fun and not at all like a soldier except that he is always dressed in all the gold braid and lace of his rank. Indeed, he does not seem to have enjoyed his task, for he opened his speech by saying, "The part of duty I am now upon is very disagreeable to my natural make and temper. . . ."

Boys and men, the Acadians huddled together. They were miserable and as silent as statues. Remember, they did not understand English. Every word Colonel Winslow spoke had to be repeated to them in French by an interpreter. Perhaps they heard few of his words, just enough to understand their doom. They must have been thinking of their homes, of their rich fields already filled with golden grain almost ready for the harvest, and of their apple orchards with the fruit heavy on the trees. They must have been thinking of their wives and mothers and sisters, and of the little children and the babies.

Colonel Winslow read on from the papers in his hands, the French interpreter repeating every word. He told the unhappy Acadians he was only obeying orders, then continued:

Therefore without hesitation I shall deliver you His Majesty's orders and instructions, namely: that your lands and tenements, cattle of all kinds and livestock of all sorts, are forfeited to the crown; with all your other effects, saving your money and household goods, and you yourselves are to be removed from this, his province. I am, through His Majesty's goodness, directed to allow you liberty to carry off your money and household goods, as many as you can without discommoding the vessels you go in.

There was much more, but it is doubtful that any Acadian there heard it. Winslow promised that families would not be separated and that the exiles would not be robbed of the things they would be permitted to take.

But what could they take? The part about money was a hideous joke. Few of them had any money, and those who did had very little. How much household goods could a man carry? And how much would he be allowed to carry? The document warned that they must not take so much that it would discommode—crowd or weigh down—the ships that were to carry them away. Actually almost everything they owned was gone—their land and homes, their cattle and crops.

All this was to be turned over to the British. They were not to be repaid for these properties in any way.

And where were they to be sent? Winslow was vague about this. He said only that he hoped ". . . in whatever part of the world you may fall you may be faithful subjects, a peaceable and happy people."

That could mean only one thing. They were to be taken to other British colonies, separated, torn apart from their own people in small groups. Winslow had promised that families would not be separated, but how could they be sure the English would keep this promise?

Then Winslow ended his speech. All the men and boys there, he told them, must remain under guard of the British troops. They must remain so until the time came for them to leave. They could not even go home to tell the women and girls of their fate. They were prisoners of the King!

Great excitement broke out then in the Church of St. Charles, and in all the other churches where the same thing was taking place. Some of the men shouted and cursed. Others wept. But there was nothing they could do. They had been forced to come to the churches unarmed. At this very moment British soldiers were searching their cabins and cottages, seizing all their rifles and shotguns and ammunition and anything that might be used as a weapon.

At Grandpré the men and boys pleaded with Winslow, and at last he allowed them to go back to their homes, twenty at a time, to tell the terrible news to the women, and to look for the last time upon their homes and belongings and pets. Winslow assured the return of those allowed to leave by telling them the lives of those still at the church depended upon their return. This was the last time some of them saw their families.

It is said the women were calmer about it than the men. It may be that some of them found it unbelievable and still hoped the British would change their minds. It may be simply that the women knew there was nothing they could do. Most of them went to work quietly, taking on much of their husbands' labor, as well as continuing with their own. They had to feed their children and themselves. Unless they worked they would starve.

As the days passed some families almost did starve. Then Winslow allowed a few men to be released so they could work the mills and provide bread for the population. But most of the men and boys he kept locked up in the church. They were so stunned with grief that, day and night, they sat in almost complete silence.

Winslow wrote a letter to Murray in which he said, "Things are as well as we could expect, and the people as easy as I should be were I in their case." He added that thirty-four heads of families were sick, and that he had had very few attempts at escape among his group.

The people of Grandpré, however, seem to have been the quietest of all the sentenced groups. Murray reported that there had been much trouble at Annapolis. Many had run away and had to be tracked down. He added, "I am afraid there will be some lives lost before they are got together. You know our soldiers hate them, and if they can find a pretense to kill them they will. . . ."

At Annapolis and elsewhere some of the men and boys escaped and whole families—husbands and wives and children and old people—fled into the woods. When this happened, English soldiers first drove off the fowl and cattle of the runaways, and then set fire to their homes and crops. This was done to prevent any sneaking back at night in order to find food.

In the woods many starved or died of illness and exposure. Some came back and surrendered as prisoners. A few of the strongest made their way to the camps of the Micmacs, who fed them and hid them from the British. Some even managed to escape into Canada and join relatives there.

All the property left behind was burned. Perhaps the most awful damage took place at Cumberland. Here the British burned 253 homes and turned wheat, flax and hay over to the roaring flames.

Outside the churches where the men and boys were imprisoned, many of the women and small children came in the evenings to kneel in prayer and beg to see their husbands, fathers and sons. It was almost impossible for them to believe that they were to be taken away, never to see Acadia again.

6 *The March to the Sea*

Some of the men did not have too long a wait in their churches. On September 10th the doors of the little church at Grandpré swung open and British officers and soldiers entered. With them was one of the Acadians' own priests. He stood there, murmuring words of comfort as the prisoners breathed fresh air for the first time in days. But the British soon became impatient. One hundred and sixty-one young men were ordered outside. The older men and boys were left behind.

As they walked out into the blinding sunlight and were ordered to fall into line, the young men must have been stunned with the realization of what was about to happen. They were being separated from the others, from their fathers and younger brothers, perhaps even from their wives and mothers and sweethearts! Anger and fear swept through the ranks.

"I will not go anywhere without my father!" one shouted.

"I want my little brother with me!" another pleaded.

"Where is my wife?" cried a third.

Women and children struggled to reach the men,

The British ignored them and prodded them with rifles to drive them on.

"You lied to us!" the men cried. "You promised we would not be separated from our families!"

but were held back by the British soldiers

Women and children came running. They struggled to reach the men, but were held back by the soldiers. With tears streaming down their cheeks, old mothers fought with British officers to reach their sons.

The march of these young men to the waiting ships is a story that has been handed down from generation to generation for two hundred years. We are told that it was a beautiful day: the sky blue, the sun bright and golden, the grass still green, the trees dripping scarlet and gold leaves.

The women followed the men, the children running at their heels. They cried and prayed as they ran, both women and children. A girl fell in the road, sobbing with her face in the dirt, while the others walked around her or stepped over her gently. Some of the women had brought pitiful bundles of clothing, loaves of bread wrapped in cloth, baskets of apples. They tried to get these to the men, but usually the women were pushed out of reach by the soldiers. Some tossed their bundles and the men tried to catch them.

At the blue water's edge the boats waited. The soldiers raised their muskets. The men marched up the gangplanks, some ordered to board this boat, others that.

"Where are they taking you, Pierre?" a woman shouted.

"Do you know where you are going, Jean?" another shrieked.

The men could not answer. They had not been told where they were going. They would sail off, and that would be the end. How could they ever find their families again in this huge world? There was almost no chance that they would ever see each other again. Even if they were all set down somewhere in America (and they were not even sure of that) how could they find each other in all this tremendous, wild and unknown continent? We must remember that in those days there were no railroads, no roads, no telegraph systems. There was almost no means of communication over far distances and no way to travel except by horseback, boat, or on foot.

Longfellow wrote of this scene in *Evangeline,* describing how Evangeline watched Gabriel, to whom she was about to be married, and Basil, his father, being led toward the ships:

So unto separate ships were Basil and Gabriel carried,
While in despair on the shore Evangeline stood with her father.
Half the task was not done when the sun went down, and the twilight
Deepened and darkened around; and in haste the refluent ocean
Fled away from the shore, and left the line of the sand-beach
Covered with waifs of the tide, with kelp and the slippery sea-weed.

This was only the beginning. For weeks and months the enforced exodus went on. In many cases the English in charge seem to have made an honest effort to see that families boarded the same ship. But in other cases they were careless, and there was much confusion. As a result there were many separations of families and sweethearts.

As the ships came in the British moved with great haste, rounding up part of a village or the people living on a group of farms. These persons were herded together like cattle, but the Acadians would surely have treated their cattle with greater kindness. Now they were hysterical, shouting and weeping, trying to carry everything they could with them.

Because many English soldiers hated the Acadians, there was much deliberate cruelty. Bundles were torn from their backs and tossed into the sea or on the beaches. If a child strayed from its mother and was lost in the crowds a British soldier might not bother to search for it or allow the mother to do so. As Longfellow told it:

There disorder prevailed, and the tumult and stir of embarking.
Busily plied the freighted boats; and in the confusion
Wives were torn from their husbands, and mothers, too late, saw their children
Left on the land, extending their arms, with wildest entreaties.

The world was not to witness scenes as dreadful as this one until almost two hundred years later. The cruelties inflicted on the Jews and other minority groups in Hitler's Germany before and during World War II, and the sorrows of the "displaced persons," are recent and similar examples of mass suffering.

Records were so badly kept at that time that we do

not know exactly how many Acadians marched to the sea from all the settlements of Acadia. Historians place the number at between 5,000 and 7,000 men, women, and children. The rest, of a population set at about 9,200 at the time of the arrest of the men by the English, escaped. Some of the people died in the woods, some remained with the Indians and in time became more Indian than French, and the rest managed to reach French Canada.

But even those who did reach Canada suffered greatly there. The government, although it was French, was not pleased to have all these people to feed. We are told they gave the escaped Acadians boiled hides and horsemeat to eat and that many of them died of starvation. Only those taken into the homes of friends, and they were few, could survive. There was no organized charity then such as we have today. There was no Red Cross, which now takes care of people in that kind of trouble.

Nations were cruel then. They still are in many ways, but at least many of us condemn their cruelties. We do not take the treatment given people such as the Acadians without complaint. In some ways it was not so then.

Historians tell us that in 1689 the French, who then owned those parts of the New World now known as northern New York and Albany, planned to exile all the inhabitants. Orders to this effect were sent by the King of France to the Count de Frontenac in Montreal. He was to arrest all the citizens of northern New York who were not loyal to France. After being separated, they were to be distributed in other parts of the New World so that they could never unite again to give France trouble. This was never done because the people suspected of disloyalty had become too powerful. The French, therefore, abandoned the plan.

The exile of the Acadians did not even cause too much excitement in France, for the King would have done the same thing himself in the same circumstances. Besides, France was busy with other matters. Another war with England was about to start.

Then, too, Louis XV and his government were corrupt. The French Court was a nest of intrigue, religious quarrels and jealousies among those straining for power. So France seems to have ignored the matter, or at least to have agreed that England was perfectly right to treat the Acadians as she pleased. After all, they were on British soil and had been considered disloyal to Britain.

Many historians have made the British treatment of the Acadians seem justified. Actually, as in any situation when there is trouble between two peoples, both sides can argue that they are right.

From their point of view the British had to get rid of the Acadians as part of England's ambition to increase her power in the New World and to enlarge the British Empire. From the Acadians' point of view they had been the first settlers in Acadia and it was theirs. On the other hand, the English argued that John and Sebastian Cabot, Englishmen, had discovered the province long before a French explorer had set foot on it.

No matter which side was right, the means used were wrong. The Acadians were robbed of their property. Through cruelty, either deliberate or careless, they were torn from one another not only as a people, but as family members. There was not even much done to see that they had food or proper clothing, or any other necessary provisions. No one cared about them, not even their own France, to whom they had been loyal through all the generations they had lived in Acadia.

So these people were taken down to the ships and

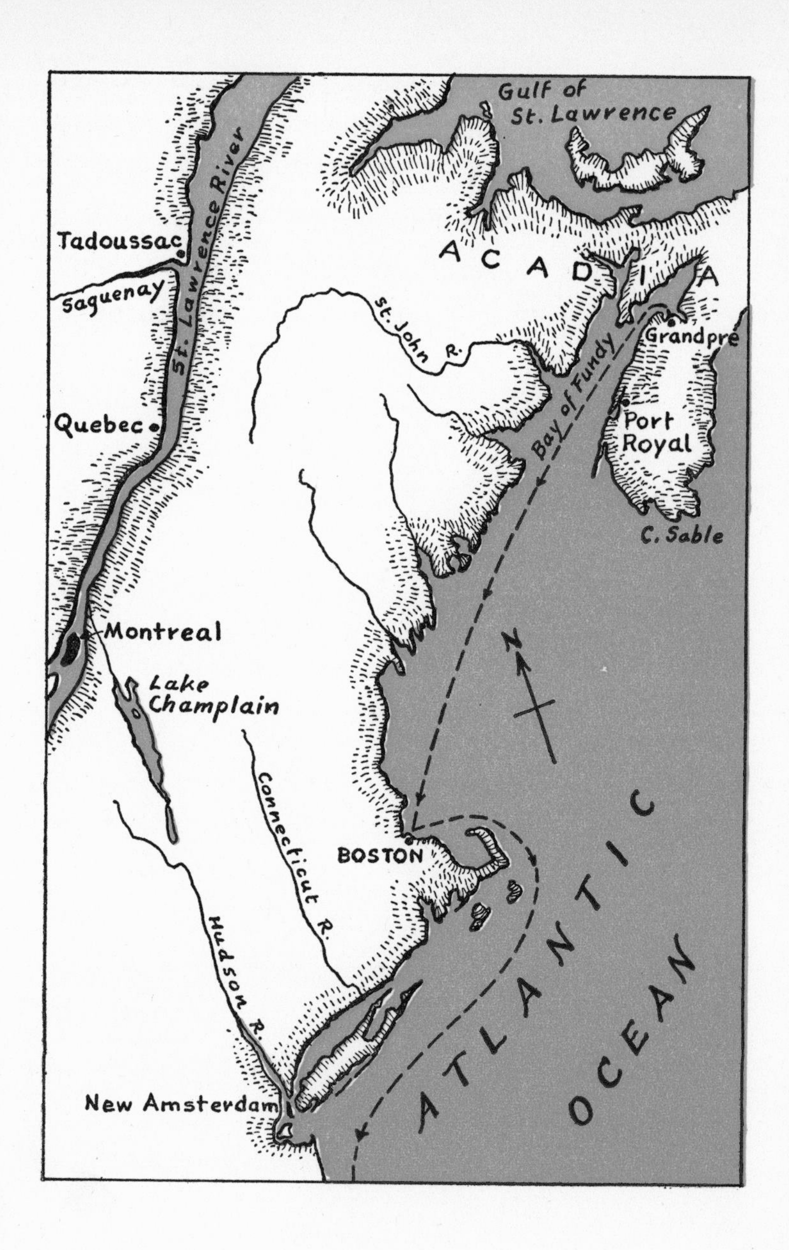
Gulf of St. Lawrence
ACADIA
Tadoussac
Saguenay
St. Lawrence River
St. John R.
Grandpre
Bay of Fundy
Quebec
Port Royal
C. Sable
Montreal
N
Lake Champlain
Connecticut R.
BOSTON
Hudson R.
ATLANTIC
OCEAN
New Amsterdam

put aboard, and the ships sailed away. An Acadian on one ship might find that his wife or parents or children were on another ship. When the vessels reached the open sea they went in different directions, stopped at different places. No Acadian knew where he was going, or where he would be put ashore on the long, changing coast of America.

7 *Into the Unknown*

AS THE TRANSPORTS LEFT GRANDPRÉ THE BROKEN-hearted Acadians leaned against the railings of the little sailing vessels, their gaze set upon their homeland for the last time. Suddenly, they saw flames break out and roar toward the sky. The English soldiers had set fire to many of the cottages and barns. This was done to warn the Acadians that they could never come back. There would be nothing left to which they might return.

The ships passed out of the rivers and bays and into the wide spaces of the Atlantic Ocean. Now they were really on their way. Rumors swept through the groups on each ship. Where were they going? The most hopeful thought perhaps they would be sent to a French colony, where they would be among people of their own kind, where they would hear their own language. Perhaps it would be the French West Indies? Perhaps

New Orleans, then under French control and the capital of Louisiana? The more gloomy thought they might be taken to some British colony to which those who broke the law in England were sent.

Many did not think about it at all. They sat like dumb animals, some of them with their faces in their hands. Where were their parents, their children, their husbands or wives? Where were their friends? Where was the man or girl with whom one was in love? Thus Evangeline wondered about Gabriel, and Gabriel about Evangeline.

Some had faint glimmerings of returned hope. Would they all meet again some place? Perhaps they would all be put off at the same place. Even if it turned out to be a kind of prison, at least they would all be together.

But that was not to be. The captain of each ship had certain papers and certain orders. The English had no idea of allowing the Acadians to reunite and to become once more a strong and dangerous enemy. However, letters were sent to governors of the colonies along the Atlantic coast, asking that the prisoners be allowed to remain in each colony where they were set down. It was thought that if they were broken into small groups, the Acadians could do no harm and might even become good British subjects.

Meanwhile, there was much misery aboard the ships. Rations were short and soon the bundles of food some

Some of the miserable Acadians slept out on the decks

of the unhappy Acadians had been allowed to bring were gone. They were fed hard dry bread and salt pork, the regular sea rations of the period. Illness broke out on some ships. There were no doctors and no medicines.

Not even the most common comforts were to be found on the crowded vessels. The Acadians slept out on the decks, on the rough wooden boards or below, huddled together in the most unsanitary conditions. Many of them hardly cared whether they lived or died. And some did die aboard the ships.

When they reached Boston, some of the ships docked and the Acadians aboard were driven ashore and allowed to rest on the common. But Boston would not have them. The Puritans there, who had helped exile them from Nova Scotia—Winslow himself was a Puritan—did not want them on their hands to feed and house and clothe. The Acadians were of a different nationality, a different religion, and spoke another language. The Puritans saw no reason why they should take charge of them and have them in their care. The general court of Boston suggested that they be taken back to Halifax and that it was the duty of the government there to care for them. Some were allowed to stay in Massachusetts, but others were put aboard the ships once more and again the ships sailed.

In Pennsylvania the attitude was better. The Quakers agreed to care for 2,000 of the Acadians. The state government allotted a sum of money—7,500 pounds—for their support, and many of the good Quakers took displaced Acadians into their homes. The Quakers have always helped the unfortunate, and are doing so to this day.

The ships containing the others moved on. There were stops at ports in Virginia, where some were set ashore. Others were put off along the coasts of South Carolina and Georgia. At last the ships were all emptied, and their crews turned them about and headed for the return trip north. Now the Acadians were distributed in a half dozen places, hundreds of miles apart from one another. At last the British felt safe.

The journey was over, there was soil beneath their feet once more, but the unhappiness of the Acadians had never been greater. The last hope they had held of being reunited was gone. No group knew where another had been landed. They could only guess that the others had been put off somewhere along the Atlantic seaboard, too.

But between the settled areas stretched mountains, swamps, and thick forests. There was almost no way to get word from one place to another except by sea or by some brave traveler between the colonies. The Acadians did not know how to write. They could not even speak

One group was set ashore along the coast of Georgia

the language of the English among whom they were now expected to live. So they clung to one another, foreigners in a foreign land.

They had just cause for unhappiness for another reason, too. They were still among the English, who had separated them from their loved ones. They hated the very sound of the English language. They hated to eat English bread, to accept English food. They did not want pity or charity from the enemy who had driven them from their homes.

Some worked to feed themselves and their families, if luckily their families were with them. They hired themselves to farmers and tilled English soil, but they disliked every moment of this toil. They had had their own farms, their own land and cattle and fowl. Now they must work for Englishmen in order to eat. Many refused to work. Sullen and always angry, they snatched what bread and other food was given them and struggled to remain alive without doing anything that would help the English in any way.

Hatred is returned with hatred. As the Acadians showed their dislike, some of the English, in turn, disliked them more and more. They said the Acadians were not only ungrateful but also lazy, and little more than charity cases upon their hands. But other Englishmen in the colonies felt sorry for the injustice the Acadians had received and tried to help them.

Too, as much as possible, the Acadians remained unto themselves. They refused to try to learn the language. Whatever differences and quarrels they had ever had among themselves were now forgotten. They were as close to each other as if they had all been one family. They would punish their children if they heard them use an English word. They would not allow them to go to school because it was taught in English and by the English. They had never thought schooling necessary, anyway. Even if an Englishman made an attempt at friendship with one of them he found his effort unreturned.

We can understand all of this feeling, but of course none of it helped the Acadians. No people like a group who stay apart and are not only different, but deliberately remain different from the others among whom they live.

Some of the Acadians went as far as they could to make themselves a burden to the English colonies. Most historians agree they did this in the hope that they would be allowed to escape, that in the end the English would be glad to be rid of them.

Remember that the Acadians were not a lazy people. They had always been hardworking and industrious when they had lived in their own homes in Acadia. What now seemed to be laziness was the result of their unhappiness and their bitterness against the English. But it was also part of a plan to get their freedom, for they were dreaming of going elsewhere—to the West Indies, to Louisiana, to any place that was French. Some were even planning to go to France, whence their forefathers had come.

8 *The Struggle for Freedom*

THE ACADIANS WERE NOT ALLOWED TO WANDER ABOUT as they pleased in all the colonies. At first they were not even allowed to work in some places, even when they wanted to work. In Virginia, for instance, they were kept under lock and key. Crowds of them were herded into a warehouse at Williamsburg and guarded by soldiers. Little food and the other necessities of life were provided them. Many became ill and died under these conditions. At last the women and young children were released. The men were kept prisoners longer.

The long winter passed. There were heavy snows and much suffering. The truth was that the Virginia authorities did not know what to do with these people. They were half afraid of them.

As the Acadians grew more and more bitter and showed their hatred in a thousand ways, the Virginians wanted only to be rid of them. Citizens complained that the Acadians set a bad example for their slaves. They tended to be friendly with the Negroes. They would not cooperate in any way and they returned even kindness with anger—not that there was much kindness shown them by the authorities. Some individuals and families did help them, perhaps as much as they could under the circumstances.

Many of the officials and some of the prominent planters in Virginia were furious that England had sent these people to be in their charge. This was twenty years before the Revolution, but already there were those who had no love for England and the crown. The beginnings of ideas about a free America and what would become the United States were already stirring. The unloading of the Acadians was considered by some wealthy Virginians only another injustice done to them by the government in London.

Ten years later, in 1765, Virginia would be the first of the thirteen colonies to protest and resist English tyranny. Even earlier most of its residents thought of themselves not as Englishmen but as Virginians.

So an idea came to the Virginia officials. Why not

send the Acadians to England? She was always demanding young men of Virginia to fight her endless wars. Let her use the Acadian men instead.

When the Acadians learned of this plan their feelings about it were mixed. Some did not care, a few ran away to hide in the woods, others saw a chance of getting back to France. At least England was closer to France.

The ships carrying the Acadians set out from Virginia early in 1756. It turned out to be the most terrible ordeal these people had yet endured. During the months they were at sea conditions were worse than they had been on the journey from Nova Scotia down the Atlantic coast. The Acadians were badly fed, crowded together without mercy. Scurvy and other diseases attacked them. Many died during the voyages, especially old people and children. One ship, the *Excelsior,* went down, with a loss of over 300 Acadian lives.

But at last about 1,200 persons reached England. They were placed under arrest at once and locked up in Newgate and other prisons. Once more their dream of freedom vanished. The Seven Years' War between England and France had broken out. They would be prisoners until it was over. Perhaps they would never see France!

Yet during the next few years other Acadians from other colonies did reach France. They begged passage whenever they had an opportunity. Some arrived late in 1755, just a few months after they had been exiled from Acadia, and they continued to come during the years that followed.

Numbers of Acadians found passage on ships going to other places. A few hundred managed to find their way to the French West Indies, principally to San Domingo. Others reached French Guiana. For a while these people were happier than most of the rest. They were on French soil. Their language was spoken. Although they grieved for those from whom they had been separated, they felt more at home than they had in English colonies. It seemed they might be able to build new lives.

The Acadians in England languished in prison for seven years. A very few escaped and managed to reach France. There they awaited the release of those still imprisoned.

The English government was not pleased to keep all these people in prison. It was expensive. Moreover, they were increasing in number all the time, as new babies were born. Yet there was nothing the British could do. The prisoners were French, and England was at war with France, so they had to be held as prisoners of war. If they were turned loose and allowed to go to France, many of them would have taken up arms against the British.

Finally, during the last years of the Seven Years' War, some of them were released from prison. These were put to work on English farms and in other ways. This was a little better for both the English and the Acadians. The English found them sometimes useful. The Acadians themselves were able to lead more normal and more healthful lives. Yet even then they had to be watched and kept under guard.

The dream of Acadia lingered. They wanted a home of their own once more—in France, or any place where they could be together. Perhaps some of them wanted revenge on the English. They were only human and they could not forget all they had suffered—their homes and crops burned, the bodies of their relatives and friends left on the beaches of Nova Scotia, the others who had died and been tossed into the lashing seas in sacks.

Like those left behind in the colonies along the Atlantic coast of America, they waited their chance. Just across the narrow English Channel there was France. And they knew a war must always come to an end.

9 *The Wandering of Evangeline*

In the meantime the Acadians who had remained in Georgia, in the Carolinas, in Maryland, and in the other colonies continued to be a nuisance. A few did become a part of the life of those places, acquiring land and starting farms, or going into business.

Occasionally there would be a marriage between an Acadian and a person from an English family. But such instances were rare. Most of the Acadians would disown the members of their race who took such a step, and the English-speaking citizens were scarcely less lenient in their attitude. They did not approve of their sons or daughters marrying these French people. Nor were they friendly toward the Acadians who began farming or doing business in their communities.

Gradually some of the Acadians began to disappear. When they vanished, neither the authorities nor the residents bothered to search for them. They were too expensive to feed, and in most cases they were considered a good riddance.

Some of those who wandered off managed to board ships for the Indies, even for France. Others simply took to the woods. Often they faced terrifying hardships and many perils. They starved or were killed by wild beasts or by unfriendly Indians.

Yet they continued to go. Freedom is more precious than life to many people, and the Acadians felt strongly about it. For this reason, they were willing to risk the terrors of the wilderness and the almost unknown country west of the colonies.

Then, during these years, they remembered the one place that might be the answer to their hopes. This was the French colony that has since become the state of Louisiana. The Acadians knew that its capital, New Orleans, far away at the mouth of the Mississippi River, was in the hands of the only government they recognized, that of France. In Louisiana their language was spoken, the people were of their blood. In fact, a few Acadians had reached New Orleans some years before. Others were by now settled along the banks of the Mississippi. This might be their new home.

When the great pilgrimage to the south began they

had been exiled from Acadia for nearly ten years. Almost a fever to get to New Orleans swept through them. Somehow—through traveling hunters and trappers, perhaps—the word went out to Acadians in Massachusetts, in Pennsylvania, in all the colonies farther to the south. They would take to the waters of the Mississippi in boats, to journey its dangerous length to their new home.

In the year 1764 they began to leave the British colonies in large numbers.

They were not held back. Indeed, many were helped

They took to the waters of the Mississippi in boats

to go. The British authorities and citizens gave them provisions and supplies, as well as guns with which to protect themselves and to provide additional food along the way.

It is probably with this group that Longfellow imagined his heroine, Evangeline, traveling at last. Searching for her sweetheart Gabriel, she had already traveled to many places trying to find him:

> *Sometimes she lingered in towns, till, urged by the fever within her,*
> *Urged by a restless longing, the hunger and thirst of the spirit,*
> *She would commence again her endless search and endeavor;*
> *Sometimes in churchyards strayed, and gazed on the crosses and tombstones . . .*

Evangeline had wondered many times if Gabriel might not be dead, as so many of her people were after ten years of exile. But she did not give up her search. Word reached her through hunters and trappers that Gabriel was in Louisiana. With a group of other Acadians she set out for that faraway land. As Longfellow tells it:

It was the month of May. Far down the Beautiful River,
Past the Ohio shore and past the mouth of the Wabash,
Into the golden stream of the broad and swift Mississippi,
Floated a cumbrous boat, that was rowed by Acadian boatmen.
It was a band of exiles: a raft, as it were, from the shipwrecked
Nation, scattered along the coast, now floating together,
Bound by the bonds of a common belief and a common misfortune;
Men and women and children, who, guided by hope or by hearsay,
Sought for their kith and their kin among the few-acred farmers
On the Acadian coast, and the prairies of fair Opelousas.
With them Evangeline went, and her guide, the Father Felician.

Of course we know now that Longfellow's great poem was for the most part a work of his imagination and that all the facts and the description he used were not precisely correct. That is the right of a poet. Yet many details were accurate.

A number of Acadians had reached New Orleans in January, 1765. A young man such as Gabriel could very easily have been among them. Others arrived almost constantly until May, the time at which Longfellow places Evangeline's journey down the river. A girl like Evangeline, coming in search of her Gabriel, may have been on a raft arriving at that time. Without a doubt there were numerous people looking for each other in all the groups of Acadians making those long hard trips.

We know now, too, how Longfellow came to write *Evangeline*. He had heard what was supposedly a true story of a girl exactly like Evangeline.

Nearly a hundred years after the Acadians had been driven from Nova Scotia, a man named George Mordaunt Haliburton came down from there to live in Boston. His wife told the story of Evangeline to her minister, the Reverend Horace Lorenzo Conolly. Dr. Conolly was later transferred to Salem, where he soon became an intimate friend of the great American writer, Nathaniel Hawthorne.

One night Hawthorne took Dr. Conolly to dinner with Longfellow at Craigie House. During the evening, Dr. Conolly told Longfellow how he had been urging Hawthorne to write this Acadian story. But somehow Hawthorne never did use the story. Some years later Longfellow asked him if he might use it as the basis of a poem, and Hawthorne consented. That is how *Evangeline* came to be written.

10 *France and the Acadians*

When the Seven Years' War ended in 1763 with the Treaty of Paris, the imprisoned Acadians in England were released. The English tried to hold them for a short time afterwards, but the new French ambassador to England, De Nivernois, demanded that they be set free. They crossed the Channel at once and reached France, the homeland of their ancestors.

At first the French authorities seem to have been proud of these people who had been so loyal to France. It was remembered that they had refused to take any oath of allegiance to England and that they had suffered because they were of French blood.

So their first welcome was a warm one. Plans were made to help them create new homes and build new lives. They were promised a grant of land upon which they might farm, or a dole. The latter was a sum of money to be given them regularly until they could find a way to support themselves.

Long before this, in 1755, when the first Acadians had begun to arrive in France, the government had started the payment of six *sols* a day to each adult among them. Children and nuns received twice that amount. A *sol* was a small copper coin worth about a penny. At that time, however, the amounts given the Acadians were considered enough to keep them from starving, at least until they found work. In addition, the French government paid the expenses of transporting all those who came from England. Later it also paid the fares of some sailing to France from America.

The Acadians landed at the ports of Cherbourg and Rochefort, and almost all of them settled in towns and cities in Normandy and Brittany, two provinces from which most of their ancestors had come. Here some of them found relatives, old family friends, and people very much like themselves. For a time at least they felt at home.

But, after waiting a while for the Acadians to decide what they wanted to do, the French government began to be displeased. For one thing, it did not want the newcomers to remain in the cities of France. At that time great numbers of farmers and country folk were moving to the cities. The government was worried that the farms were being deserted. Besides, the city streets were filled with beggars. Unable to find work, the country folk often turned to begging.

With the Acadians added to the already crowded cities, the situation became worse. In 1763 it was said there were more than one hundred thousand beggars on the streets of French cities. This number was growing larger each day.

It had been eight long years since the Acadians had left Nova Scotia. They had been farmers then, but not all wanted to return to farming. Too, some who had been children when they were first exiled were now grown men and women. These people could hardly remember Acadia, and they had never been trained for farm work. Most of them had grown up in English prisons.

On the other hand, they were not trained for anything. With no education, they seldom could find work of any kind in the towns and cities. They had to live on their six *sols* a day, and on the charity of others. The government wondered what it could do about the problem.

The years passed. Some Acadians drifted to the country and went to work on farms. Others became fishermen along the coasts of Normandy. But most of them remained in the crowded cities, barely keeping alive. They became unhappier all the time. So did the French authorities. They began making plans to get the Acadians out of the cities and to find some way in which they might become self-supporting.

Then in 1770 the Marquis de la Marche suggested that a large colony of Acadians be settled on Corsica. France had just become ruler of that big island off the coast of Italy, the same island where Napoleon Bonaparte had been born just the year before. The island land was fertile, the fishing was fine. It was planned that each family would be given a few acres of land, tools and animals.

But every Acadian turned down this offer. They would not go. They did not want to live in Corsica, which was really Italian and not French. The French government withdrew the offer. Some historians have said they did so with relief because to have carried it out would have been extremely expensive.

In 1773 eight Acadian families went to the Isle of Jersey in the English Channel. They were given land

and houses. In a short time all were dropped from the dole list and no more has ever been known of them. Probably their descendants remained there forever.

A little later seventy-eight families went to Belle Ile off the coast of Brittany. Seventy-eight houses were built for them and each family was given land, a cow or two, and chickens. These, too, gradually became self-supporting.

In 1774 the Marquis de Perusse, a rich landowner, offered homes and work to 1,500 Acadians on his property in the Province of Poitou. The plan was that five villages would be built. In each village there would be thirty houses. Each house would be the home of ten Acadians. They would be given house furnishings, animals and tools. Their work would be to clear the thick woods covering the land and to turn it into farm and grazing land. The French government agreed to pay part of the expenses. The Acadians accepted this offer, and 1,500 of them were selected to work for the Marquis.

But this lasted less than one year. Only fifty-eight houses were built when the Acadians began to drift away. In no time at all they were back in the cities. Only a few families remained.

We do not know why they left. The Marquis, in a rage, said they were too lazy to work and that they were ungrateful, but they may have had other reasons.

Years later, in 1791, when France was in the throes of the French Revolution, a speaker in the National Assembly said the Acadians had received terrible treatment from the Marquis de Perusse. Numbers of the men selected for the clearing of those forests had been too old for the work. They could not chop down trees. Many had died of hard work and hunger on the rich estate of the Marquis, for they had been given little food. Some of the Acadians, this speaker added, had been born rich men in the land from which they had come. They could not live as the Marquis had expected.

We do not know now if this is entirely true. Yet there must have been some truth in the story. It is hard to believe the Acadians would have preferred their miserable lives in the towns if the Marquis had given them a real chance to make homes for their large families.

Probably we can take it for granted that the French aristocrats who were in power before the Revolution did not offer the Acadians much work that they could do. Probably the Marquis wanted slaves for his estate, and probably he placed little value upon their lives.

More and more the Acadians came to believe that they were being mistreated. They still received their tiny allowance of money from the government, but it was not enough. Too, they had steadily come to realize they were not at home in France after all.

None of them had been born there. It was true that they were of French blood and spoke the French language, but in no other way were they like the people among whom they lived. The Acadians were from the New World and this was the Old. They were still foreigners.

It was as early as 1772 when the Acadians in France began to hear of Louisiana. Some of their own relatives were there, they learned. Ships arriving from New Orleans brought news and messages. The Acadians discovered that Louisiana was becoming the second home of their people. Life was good there. Fertile soil could be had for the asking and the taking. Its people enjoyed more freedom than could be found in Europe.

Most of the Acadians had been in France for nine years, and some longer, but now they turned their heads toward the New World once more. Perhaps Louisiana was the answer to all their problems.

There was one serious difficulty. Louisiana, long

French territory, now belonged to Spain. France had given Louisiana to Spain in 1762. But this did not matter to the Acadians. Their friends in Louisiana described

Fifteen hundred Acadians left France for New Orleans

the place as being very French in spite of the Spanish ownership. The French language was spoken. The Spanish officials were not severe. Aid would be given to anyone coming there.

But the French government ignored the first requests from the Acadians that they be allowed to go to Louisiana. France did not like the idea of any of her subjects going to live under Spanish rule. In 1775 many of those returning from the land of the Marquis de Perusse asked once more for permission to go to Louisiana. Again they were refused. War had broken out again between France and England, and the French authorities considered it dangerous to allow the Acadians to go.

More years passed. In 1784 the Acadians tried again. That year they sent secret messages to the Count of Aranda, who was then powerful in the Spanish government. The Count took up the matter with the French officials.

France agreed to let the Acadians go, but under certain conditions. Spain was to pay all the costs of sending the Acadians across the seas. Spain was also to give them land, animals and tools, and pay them a small amount of money until they became self-supporting. Spain, anxious to settle Louisiana, agreed on condition that the Acadians take an oath of allegiance to Spain before they sailed. More than 1,500 Acadians took the oath and thus became subjects of Spain.

These 1,500 Acadians sailed for New Orleans in Spanish vessels during May, 1785. They sailed with great joy. Ahead lay a new life. They would be among their own people, yet far away from Europe and France, where they had been unable to lift themselves out of poverty. Louisiana seemed to them a promised land.

11 *Evangeline on the Mississippi*

All through the winter and spring of 1765 those Acadians who had remained in America journeyed from the colonies of the eastern seaboard toward Louisiana. They had some supplies and a few were armed, but the trip was dangerous in spite of these aids. Some of the weaker among them died along the way.

There was no central starting point. Usually they traveled in small groups, some of these consisting of only a few families, and they came from all the places along the eastern seaboard where they had stopped for a while. They came from New England, from Pennsylvania, from the Carolinas, and many other places. Yet there seems to have been some kind of grapevine means of communication among them, and many of them seem to have met upon the waters of the Mississippi during this same season. And all of them seem to have been headed for the same destination, which was

New Orleans. They headed southward in a steady swarm, almost as do flocks of birds at the start of winter.

It was necessary that they first cross half the continent to the Mississippi River. This part of the trip was filled with dangers of many kinds. Then, at water's edge, they must build crude boats and rafts and take the risk of traveling slowly down the Mississippi for hundreds of miles. It took a brave people and a determined people to go through all this. All of them knew before they started that they might never reach journey's end.

Yet during those early months of 1765 the river was dotted with their rude boats. Once embarked upon the waters, they seem to have felt the worst part of the journey was over. Although some had perished in the forests, others kept coming. Like all pioneers in the New World, they had learned through necessity to brave any danger, to be patient, to endure even grief as well as possible.

Longfellow tells us of the river voyage of Evangeline and her friend, Father Felician. Behind and in front of them, as well as on either side, were other rafts and boats, all carrying Acadians. Now and then they were caught up in a swift current that hurled them onward at terrifying speed. But most of the time they floated slowly and gently southward:

> *Day after day they glided adown the turbulent river;*
> *Night after night, by their blazing fires, encamped on its borders.*

In order to avoid the currents, the boats kept as close to the shore as they dared. They also kept close to each other, so that they might be of help if a craft should turn over or someone fall into the water. From Longfellow's description, from other reports, and from our own imagination we know much of how it must have been. Boats must have sprung leaks, been overturned, and there must have been other kinds of accidents. The Acadians passed sand bars, went around green islands, and had to force their way through thick entanglements of brush and driftwood at the river's edge.

Each night they camped. Fires were built and meals cooked. Some of the men would shoot wild game or catch fish to increase their dwindling supply of food. Children would run and play around the campfires, and sometimes get lost and have to be found by frantic parents. Mothers would hold babies in their arms all night to keep them warm and safe.

The men would take turns staying awake while the others slept, for there were wildcats and bears and other animals in the forests about them. In some places there were unfriendly Indians. Deadly snakes and alligators were a constant menace.

There was almost no civilization along the banks of the Mississippi in those days, only a few trading posts and villages. There were a few forts. Now and then the travelers would reach one of these places. They would be welcomed and they might receive extra rations, fresh water, and have a chance to rest in comparative safety. Then they would push on again.

In spite of their hardship, the Acadians were far from unhappy. They were sure they would find homes at the end of the journey. It is nice to think, too, that they found some pleasure in the trip, for the scenery was wildly beautiful. They might even have had some fun, for the Acadians were by nature a gay and lighthearted people when they had a chance to be. Often they sang, on the river itself, and, when the country seemed safe from the Indians, around their fires at night. Longfellow imagined them thus:

Silent at times, then singing familiar Canadian boat-songs,
Such as they sang of old on their own Acadian rivers.
And through the night were heard the mysterious sounds of the desert,
Far off, indistinct, as of wave or wind in the forest,
Mixed with the whoop of the crane and the roar of the grim alligator.

As they moved farther south and finally neared the end of their voyage, the river banks became more picturesque. There were drooping willows and rugged oak

Often they sang around their fires at night

trees from the limbs of which moss dripped downward. The Acadians pushed their way through waters clogged with water lilies. Cypress stumps had to be avoided, and sleek black snakes called moccasins writhed past the tiny boats, causing the passengers to shudder with terror.

Nearing New Orleans, they found more signs of civilization. Here and there were cultivated fields, as well as a few houses of imposing appearance and the small log cabins of Negroes. They began to meet hunt-

Relatives came to meet them with shouts of joy

ers and trappers who would call to them from the banks of the Mississippi. Most exciting of all, the greetings were usually in French, their own language! Now and then a man on horseback would ride down to the water's edge to give them directions.

Longfellow does not take Evangeline all the way to New Orleans during her trip down the river. Instead he has her party enter Bayou Teche, an important body of water that cuts through southwest Louisiana:

> *Slowly they entered the Teche, where it flows through the green Opelousas*
> *And through the amber air, above the crest of the woodland,*
> *Saw the column of smoke that arose from a neighboring dwelling;—*
> *Sounds of a horn they heard, and the distant lowing of cattle.*

Actually, according to all accounts, most of the Acadians who traveled down the Mississippi continued on to New Orleans. They climbed the levees (mounds of earth that edged the small port and held back the river water) to gaze upon the houses and streets. Coming to meet them with shouts of joy were relatives and friends who had arrived earlier. Then all would kneel in prayers of thanksgiving.

12 *New Orleans Under the Spanish*

There was great happiness among the first Acadians to arrive in New Orleans. The language of the town was French, and so were all its habits and customs and traditions. Besides, its citizens welcomed the Acadians heartily. They opened their purses to those who came during the first half of 1765, and even took them into their homes until other arrangements could be made.

The Acadians were grateful. They had arrived at the levees of New Orleans in poverty, with little more than the clothes on their backs. In all, about 650 arrived in the city between January and the end of May. As has been said, they came slowly, sometimes in small groups, a boat or two or three at a time, small boats that carried only a few persons apiece. At other times larger numbers of boats arrived all at once, as larger groups of

Acadians had come together somewhere along the banks of the river.

Yet as still more groups who had sailed down the Mississippi arrived, it became apparent that something would have to be done about them. In 1765 the population of New Orleans was only a little more than 3,000, many of whom were Negro slaves. For the remaining portion to support and take care of all these extra persons was impossible. By the end of May no one had room left to take care of the Acadians who were still coming into the city. Besides, as time went on, most of the Acadians themselves became restless. They wanted to form their own community, to be together.

It was then suggested that the refugees be sent to form settlements in Attakapas and Opelousas, regions in the bayou country, much of it prairie country and fertile farmland, districts southwest of New Orleans, which have now been divided into parishes with other names. Land was theirs for the taking and they were aided in gathering together tools and supplies so that they might build themselves homes and begin farms. It was predicted that within a few years these com-

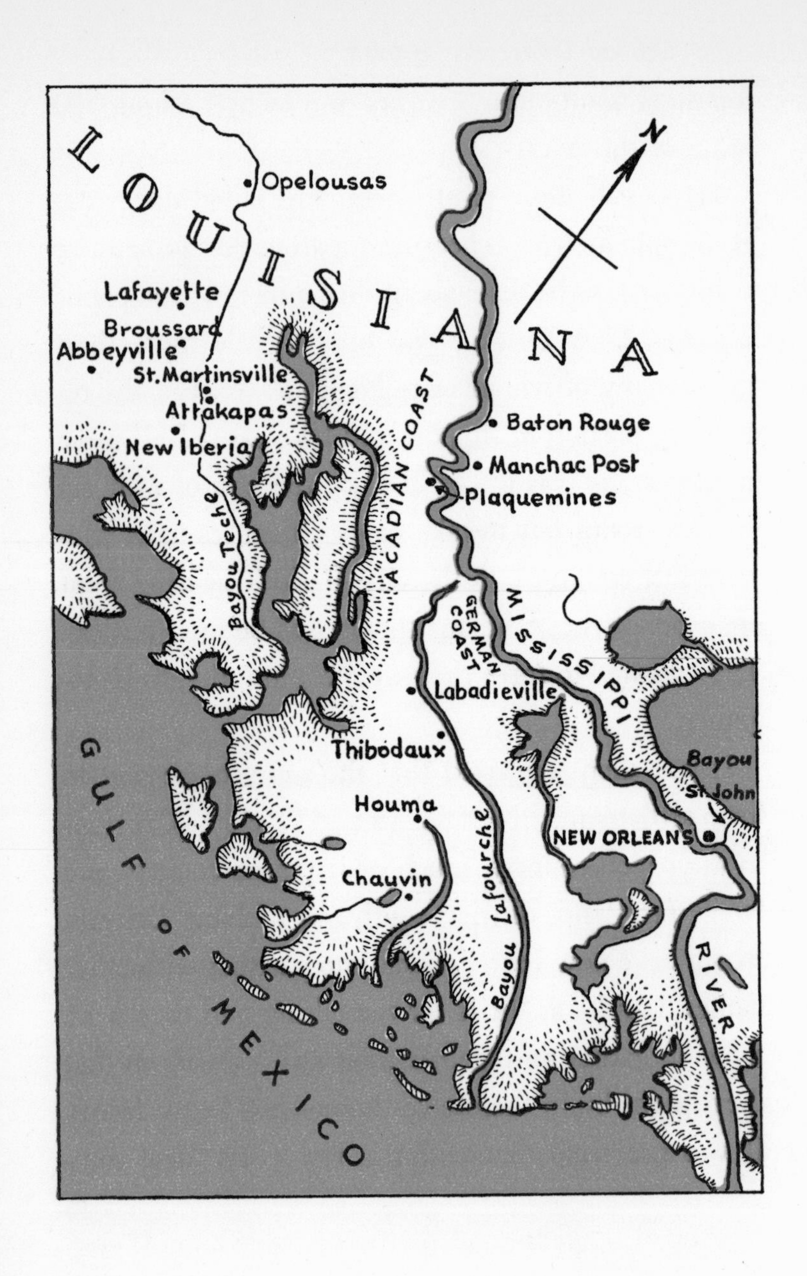
LOUISIANA
N
Opelousas
Lafayette
Broussard
Abbeyville
St. Martinsville
Attakapas
New Iberia
Bayou Teche
ACADIAN COAST
Baton Rouge
Manchac Post
Plaquemines
GERMAN COAST
MISSISSIPPI
Labadieville
Thibodaux
Houma
Chauvin
Bayou Lafourche
Bayou St. John
NEW ORLEANS
RIVER
GULF OF MEXICO

munities would be self-supporting and prosperous. Although the government of Louisiana had very little money, it gave the Acadians what it could. Private persons added whatever they could afford.

Most of the Acadians were happy to have this opportunity to make homes, and they moved to the regions suggested. Only a few remained in the city. Some of these were women without husbands who had small children. Others were old people who felt they were no longer strong enough to begin farming.

No more Acadians arrived until February, 1766. During that month 216 more appeared on the levees. These were happy to follow the example of the others. They made their homes on what was called the German Coast and as far north as Baton Rouge. Like the others, they were given tools and farm implements and money to keep them from starvation for a year.

One month later Don Antonio de Ulloa, the Spanish high commissioner, and his aides, arrived in New Orleans to take charge of the city.

The people of French New Orleans had almost forgotten that their town now belonged to Spain. It had been more than three years since France had given the port to Spain, and in all that time no Spanish officials had arrived. So the coming of Ulloa was a shock. The people did not like it and their protests began almost at once.

But there was no trouble for a while. The French authorities turned over the administration of the city and shortly afterwards some of them sailed for France. Others remained, including Governor Philip Aubry.

Ulloa was a mild man, but he was determined to let the citizens of New Orleans know who owned the port and the colony and to whom they must bow as their rulers. He was a patriotic Spaniard, and he had a successful career behind him. He had been an officer in the Spanish Navy, and official representative of Spain in South America, and was, in addition, a scientist of some distinction. He was a man of wit and learning, but he was also smug, arrogant, pompous, and vain.

His reception in New Orleans was sullen and cold. The people disliked him at once. Yet they were respectful upon his arrival. They grumbled among themselves, but for a while gave no outward sign of how they felt.

Spanish law became the law of the city. Spanish money took the place of French money. Ulloa had a lofty opinion of his own importance, so he treated the leading citizens of New Orleans as inferiors. Since they also had a high opinion of themselves, their dislike of Ulloa increased rapidly.

The first real trouble between Ulloa and the members of the Superior Council of New Orleans, which was made up of citizens of the city, came because of the change in money. Orleanians feared the new money would have little value. This was a very complicated matter, but Ulloa had his way in the end.

Many other things happened. The French troops in the city refused to serve under the flag of Spain. When yellow fever struck New Orleans, the misery of the town and its people was complete. Ulloa came to the rescue then. He used Spanish money to help put the city back on its feet, but he wanted repayment. He demanded that Aubry help him enforce Spanish laws in New Orleans.

Aubry tried to do this, but without much success. Most Orleanians did not like the laws—especially those concerning commerce and shipping — which they thought were all for the benefit of Spain.

Bitterness grew in the city, yet the year 1767 passed

quietly enough—on the surface. Underneath there raged a storm of anger and hatred for Ulloa.

Rumors began spreading that he was not only unjust, but also cruel. According to one rumor, he had ordered a large number of Acadians to be placed on ships and sent back to New England. Another was that he was making plans to sell other Acadians into slavery on the auction blocks. We do not know how much of this was true. Ulloa had, as a matter of fact, supplied many Acadian families with money and foodstuffs when they arrived, and had allowed them to take up land near the city.

By the spring of 1768 Orleanians were holding secret meetings at which they made plans to get rid of Ulloa and all the other Spanish officials. These meetings went on all summer and into the fall. More and more people joined the conspiracy, including many Acadians who believed Ulloa had mistreated their people. Also gathered together were German residents of New Orleans and outlying sections of the city.

During the night of October 27, 1768, the cannons guarding the city at the Spanish garrison called the Tchoupitoulas Gate were put out of order and the few soldiers there frightened away. Before dawn four hundred armed Creoles and Acadians led by a prominent Orleanian, Joseph Roy Villeré, were marching through the streets of the city. Behind them came a body of Germans joined by other male residents of the city.

Revolt swept the town. Carrying torches and flares, the revolutionists surrounded the homes of all the Spanish officials. Others stalked the streets singing patriotic French songs.

Aubry, although a Frenchman himself, gathered together his small body of troops and swore to defend Ulloa. Toward evening he managed to get Ulloa, his wife, and all the Spanish aides and officers aboard a Spanish frigate that was tied up in the river. They remained aboard while Aubry tried to talk those who had revolted into allowing the Spanish officials to return.

But the revolutionists would not listen. Three nights after the Spanish had sought refuge on the ship, it was cut loose from its moorings by a group of Acadians headed by one named Petit. The vessel drifted down the river with Ulloa and all his officials aboard. That was the last New Orleans ever saw of Don Antonio de Ulloa. He went first to Cuba, then back to Spain.

For a time after this New Orleans was free. Villeré was made temporary leader, and the Acadians and Germans returned to their farms.

Then, at dawn on July 24, 1769, many months after the forced departure of Ulloa, twenty-four Spanish men-of-war entered the mouth of the river. They arrived in the port in August, and 2,600 seasoned Spanish soldiers, led by Count Alexander O'Reilly, took over the city.

13 *The Acadians and the American Revolution*

WHEN THE WAR OF INDEPENDENCE BROKE OUT IN 1775 news of it was a long time reaching the prairies and bayou country where the Acadians in Louisiana lived, but when they heard of it they were overjoyed.

Their sympathies were with the Americans, who were now struggling for freedom as once they themselves had struggled. When France entered the war, at first with aid to the American colonies, then with an outright treaty of alliance, there was even more reason for the Acadians to be on the American side.

There was, however, no war activity in Louisiana until 1777. The American colonies were far away from Louisiana in those days, so far in time and travel that they might almost have been in Europe. It was a long time before news came, and when it did it was at best scarce and not always true.

Then, in February, 1777, Don Bernardo de Galvez

was appointed governor of Louisiana, which was still in the hands of Spain.

The new young governor, who was to become one of the most colorful figures of his time, won great popularity in Louisiana almost immediately. He began his term of office by removing the strict laws of trade and making it possible for French vessels to land at New Orleans.

And Galvez had a great dislike for the English, as all Spaniards did then. The start of the War of Independence found him eager to aid the Americans. When England and France began to fight against each other because of France's open aid to the colonies, Galvez had many of the French settlers of Louisiana, including the Acadians, on his side.

The New Orleans Creoles took no active part in the American Revolution. The Creoles, the name by which Orleanians of French and Spanish blood called themselves, had no real interest in the American colonies. However, they feared an attack by the English should the Americans lose the war, and so they wanted the colonies to win.

The Spanish officials worked hard to aid the Americans from the beginning. Regular supplies were sent

News of the American Revolution was greeted with joy

to Virginia and Pennsylvania from New Orleans. Soon the port became a nest of spies who were working on the American side. Secret agents were smuggled into the Floridas, which belonged to Great Britain, in attempts to stir up revolt against British rule. In 1779 Spain declared war upon England.

This was the chance Galvez had been awaiting. Already he had done the English much harm. He had helped in the sending of supplies and munitions to the

Americans. He had permitted the agents, especially an American named James Willing, to pillage and terrorize West Florida.

Now Galvez went into the war wholeheartedly, although not for the sake of American victory. He went into it in the hope that Spain would be victorious and thus add to her holdings in the areas near Louisiana. He called for volunteers, but he got few from among the Creoles, the city folk of New Orleans. The volunteers came from the Acadians in the outlying sections. Hundreds of young Acadian men joined eagerly with Galvez to fight against the English.

In less than a month Galvez and his men had conquered and captured Manchac, Baton Rouge and Natchez. Then he attacked Mobile and Pensacola. In May, 1781, the two Floridas—West Florida and East Florida—were added to Louisiana for Spain. Galvez's victory in that section of the hemisphere was complete. Spain felt free of the fear that England might one day try to take Louisiana away from her.

And the victory was, of course, of great aid also to the Americans. Galvez's exploits kept the English busy. They were forced to use part of their strength fighting him and his Spanish and Acadian troops.

To the Acadians it was also a great triumph. At last they had enjoyed the opportunity to fight back at their old enemy, the English. When the war was all over and England's power was forever banished from the American colonies, they felt safe at last. Never again would they know English rule.

14 *The Arrivals From France*

Twenty years after the first Acadians reached New Orleans, the families who had gone to France began to arrive. This was in 1785, and there had been many changes.

Somehow the French people of New Orleans had become accustomed to Spanish laws, Spanish money, and the Spaniards themselves. Spanish soldiers and officials had married French girls. French customs and ideas were still the rule among the residents, and everyone still spoke the French language.

Don Estevan Miro was governor of Louisiana when the Acadians from France arrived. Miro had taken the place of Galvez, and although he was a rather stern man he was not unpopular. He had begun his regime with acts of charity.

It is difficult to believe now that in those days there was much leprosy, or what was supposed to be leprosy, in Louisiana. Miro established a colony for lepers near Bayou St. John, a few miles outside of what was then the city. Here all lepers were confined. Before this they had begged in the town streets.

Doctors now think that many of these unfortunate people did not have leprosy at all, but other diseases. In any case, within a few years after Miro's establishment of the colony, leprosy almost vanished from New Orleans. Miro also added to the funds set aside for the Charity Hospital in New Orleans. This had been founded in 1735 with money left by a sailor, Jean Louis, for a hospital for the poor.

More than 1,500 Acadians had sailed from France to New Orleans. Their journey was by no means an easy one, and not all arrived. At sea they faced all the perils that were commonplace during ocean travel in those days, besides their own special problems.

They had taken an oath of allegiance to Spain and they were now Spanish subjects. Spain had paid the cost of their trip, and promised them a new home in Louisiana. But that was all. Many, after years of poverty in France, owned nothing but the clothes on their backs. They had no money. On some ships they had been almost starved on the way over. Scurvy and other diseases had attacked them. Burials had been daily occurrences at sea. Storms had lashed some vessels and cost other lives. So it was a miserable and frightened crowd of people that finally arrived in New Orleans.

Miro had wanted these Acadians from France to come to Spanish Louisiana, for he had a great desire to add to the population. As part of this plan, he imported a number of families from the Canary Islands. He even invited Americans to settle on the western bank of the Mississippi. However, he demanded that they become subjects of Spain, and few would accept this condition.

The reason for Miro's longing to see a large population in Louisiana was his fear of the growing United States. Already Americans in Kentucky and Tennessee, and in the Ohio Valley, were saying that the port of New Orleans and the Mississippi River should belong to the United States. Talk of this kind was to go on until the Louisiana Purchase in 1803. Thus Miro did all he could to strengthen the Spanish colony over which he ruled.

So he welcomed the Acadians from France with more warmth than had been given those who had arrived twenty years earlier. Some of the earlier settlers were on hand to meet the newcomers too. There were joyful reunions of relatives and friends. In a short time the horrors of their sea voyage were almost forgotten. The newcomers were granted lands near the first groups who had arrived, and they settled on both sides of the Mississippi, near Plaquemines, on Bayou Lafourche, and on Bayou Teche, in the districts of Attakapas and Opelousas.

By this time more than 4,000 Acadians had arrived in Louisiana. There were scatterings of them in other parts of the continent and a handful in France. However, the largest portion of those exiled from Nova Scotia had found a new home in southern and southwestern Louisiana.

Louisiana did truly become a new home for these people. In some ways they soon found it better than Acadia as a place to live. The climate was much milder. There were no freezing winters, no snows. The land was so fertile that food could be grown with much less effort than had been needed in Nova Scotia. The pasture land was fine for cattle. The waters of Louisiana provided shrimp and oysters, crabs and fish.

Then, during the French Revolution, other people came to southwestern Louisiana. These were titled refugees—aristocrats who had fled France to escape

The aristocrats tried to live as they had in Paris

death on the guillotine. Most of these settled in and near a little village now called St. Martinville, in the heart of the Bayou Teche country where many Acadian families had settled.

At first these aristocrats ignored the Acadians. They tried to live as they had in Paris. They gave balls at which the ladies appeared dressed in the court gowns they had managed to bring with them and covered with the jewels they had smuggled out of France. They amused themselves with fashionable country picnics, with masquerades, and they even opened a theater in which they staged operas. Soon their village was known all over the countryside and in New Orleans as *Le Petit Paris*—Little Paris.

A young girl, Suzanna Bossier, traveling through the section with her father in 1795, described *Le Petit Paris* in a letter as "a pretty little village . . . filled with barons, marquises, counts and countesses."

Most of these refugees believed they were only to stay in Louisiana for a short while, and that they would return to France. But few ever did so. Some moved to New Orleans in later years, but most of them, when what money they had was gone and their jewels were sold, took up land and turned to farming. In time their children and their children's children often intermarried with the Acadians.

In time, too, what had been *Le Petit Paris* became a thriving Acadian village. Eventually named St. Martinville, it was for years the most flourishing town on Bayou Teche and the center of Acadian life in that section. It was also a fashionable summer resort for people vacationing from New Orleans and for planters in the vicinity. The village even had an opera season and was looked upon somewhat as a center of culture.

All this, of course, was the work of outsiders and was for their pleasure. For a long time the Acadians were to remain a simple people. Life was better and easier for them once they reached Louisiana, but the struggle for survival was by no means over.

15 *At Journey's End*

THE ACADIANS HAD REACHED WHAT WAS TO BE THEIR home; their wanderings had come to an end. But, like all other pioneer people in the world's history, they still had to create homes out of the wilderness, the swamp, the jungle.

They had land, some tools, a few animals, some grain and seed—but besides these possessions they owned very little. They had, however, regained something that had not been theirs for many years—peace of mind. They felt that they were wanted, as they had not been wanted since those days long past in Acadia. They had each other. They were in a place where their language was spoken, where people practiced the same religion. These last two advantages were very important to the Acadians.

When Man moves into a wilderness the first thing he must build is shelter. So the Acadians built houses.

Those who had come first to Louisiana in 1765 erected crude shacks of logs and wild palmetto leaves as temporary homes. Then they built much stronger cabins—sometimes of wood, but more often of clay and twigs with palmetto roofs and hard-packed earth floors.

These cabins, which usually contained only one or two rooms, were similar to the adobe houses used in some parts of the West. Their walls were thick and solid, and the houses were cool in the summer and warm enough in the mild Louisiana winter. Most of them had a single door and no windows. The Acadians who arrived later, including those from France, imitated these structures. Soon the bayous of southwestern Louisiana were dotted with houses built on the same pattern.

Outbuildings appeared. People cooked in the open air. They made their own bricks, and near their houses they built fireplaces and ovens in which they baked bread and prepared other food. In a short time many people added indoor fireplaces, too—huge ones such as they had built in Acadia, where the iron pots hung from chains and where families and neighbors gathered in the evenings. Fences went up as their flocks of chickens and geese and their herds of cattle grew. In a few years it must have seemed that they had lived in Louisiana forever. It was home.

Almost everything they had they made with their hands. The men made all the furniture—benches, chairs and tables, chests, bureaus and bedsteads. Mattresses were stuffed with goose feathers or the soft moss that hung from the great live oak trees that lined the bayous. On their handmade spinning wheels and looms the women made not only clothing, but also quilts and linens, rugs and bedspreads. As the years passed, their houses, always spotless, the floors clean and dry even when made of earth, became pretty and homelike with their handicraft.

The Acadians had been a farming people, and it is probable that they had intended to remain so in Louisiana. It is certain that they continued for some time to till the soil. Each family raised most of its own vegetables, and kept its own chickens and a cow or two, if it was lucky enough to have them.

However, many began turning to other occupations, in addition to their small farms. They did this to add to the food they could put upon their tables or to trade with a neighbor for something they needed.

Fishing was in their blood, too. Had not many of

them fished in Nova Scotia? And here were the bayous and lakes teeming with all kinds of sea creatures that were good to eat—fish, crabs, shrimp, and oysters.

Numbers of the men also turned to trapping. They had trapped in Acadia and here were the Louisiana woods and swamps rich with wild life—muskrat, opossum, raccoon, mink and skunk, and other animals whose fur had great value. Today Louisiana leads the nation in the production of fur pelts. It is the Acadian trapper who brings them to the market.

The Acadians could have found no land more suitable for them than Louisiana. As Longfellow put it in *Evangeline:*

> *Beautiful is the land, with its prairies and forests of fruit-trees;*
> *Under the feet a garden of flowers, and the bluest of heavens*
> *Bending above, and resting its dome on the walls of the forest.*
> *Those who dwell there have named it the Eden of Louisiana.*

The bayou country of Louisiana, where nearly all the Acadians settled, is a beautiful part of America. It is flat, as is almost all of the state. There are no mountains, and there is not even a hill in this southwestern section. It has been said there are no rocks in Louisiana, no stones. It is almost true that there is none larger than a man can hold in his hand.

But the winding bayous, the immense oak trees, their limbs forming patterns against sky and water, the spreading pastures and prairies, the misty swamps, have an unbelievable beauty. Moss drapes the trees, and there are flowers everywhere—wild azaleas, dogwood, roses, irises, jasmines, water lilies. There is much wild bird life—a variety of ducks, herons, egrets, pelicans and the small song birds.

The Acadians always got on well with their neighbors. Not far from many places where they settled in Louisiana were colonies of Germans, and there was never any trouble between the two peoples. The Acadians seem always to have been clannish and to have made very few friends outside their own group. However, they mingled with the Germans as the years passed, and there were frequent marriages between them. This is probably one reason why there are blonde and blue-eyed Acadians on the bayous today.

Neither did they have much trouble with the Indians, any more than they had had with the Micmacs

The children played at catching shrimp and crawfish

in Acadia. In Louisiana they usually enjoyed the friendship of the Opelousa, Houma, Chitimacha, Attakapa (who are reported to have been man-eaters at one time) and the other local tribes.

They learned much from these Indians. Indeed it is likely that without the help of the Indians and their teachings, the first Acadians might not have survived.

To some extent they copied the Indian style in building their first shelters and houses. They learned from them something of the art of making pottery and baskets. The Indians taught them which of the native grains and other wild foods could be eaten, and how they could be prepared. From the Indians they learned to carve from a single tree trunk a boat called a pirogue. This is still in use today. In time the Acadians and Indians intermarried, and some Acadian families have Indian blood today.

Once their houses were built and made livable and their crops started, the Acadians must have been happy.

Missionaries performed the marriages and christenings

There was always work. The whole family was compelled to labor so that they might live, but fishing and hunting and trapping became sports to them as well as necessary parts of their lives. There was little cold weather to shut them in. So in the evenings there were dances and frolics and visits from house to house. There were no schools for the children, but parents taught them whatever was necessary for them to know to earn a living. They did not use money. They had no need of it. Their hands, their few tools, the earth and woods, gave them all they required.

A boy worked the fields with his father, or fished or trapped with him, and a girl helped her mother with the milking or the weaving or the household tasks. When the children were not busy, they had the bayous and the forests for their playgrounds. Small boys learned to guide the long, sleek pirogues through the shining waters at high speeds, and to ride on the backs of ponies across the wide, green prairies. Both boys and girls enjoyed Indian games, and played at setting traps, at catching the shrimp and the crawfish. It was an exciting and carefree life for the young.

But it was also a lonely life. For many years, for generations, the Acadians never left their bayou and prairie homes. They were cut off from the world, for few people visited them. Only rarely did they see an outsider or did one of them journey as far as New Orleans.

Possibly nowhere else in America did a people build a world so entirely their own. They remained a race set apart, mingling with their few neighbors a little, marrying some Germans and Indians, but not interested in what went on outside their region.

For a long time they had no villages nor, until St. Martinville was built up, did they group themselves into anything resembling a town.

For years they did not have even a priest of their own. Instead, missionaries traveled among them, reaching some of them only once in several months. Then all the marriages for which young couples had been waiting would be performed, all the babies that had been born would be christened, and prayers would be said over the graves of those who had died since the missionaries' last visit. Yet the Acadians remained a deeply religious people and eventually church steeples began towering over the bayous.

The few outsiders who did travel among them in the early years found them friendly, hospitable, and kind. There was nothing too good for a guest in an Acadian home. The coffee and homemade wine were always ready for the visitor, and the table was spread with food. There was gossip and music and laughter.

But when the visitor departed, the Acadian world remained the same, unchanged and untouched by this contact with the outside. The Acadians liked it that way. They lived as they pleased, according to their own habits, and at least for a long time much as they had lived in Nova Scotia. They did not want to change. What they had dreamed of had come true. They had homes, and they were together. They had peace. They wanted nothing else.

16 *The American Acadians*

IN 1802 SPAIN RETURNED THE TERRITORY OF LOUISIANA to France. This caused excitement in New Orleans when the news reached there, and the Acadians, still French at heart, were glad when they heard of it, too. Yet it made no change in their lives, and probably some of them, living in remote spots, never heard of it at all.

Of course they had all been Spanish subjects. But Spanish law never touched them, they seldom heard any language but French, and so they had never been anything but French in their habits and ways. Indeed, as the years passed they were ceasing to be even that. They were developing customs of their own, traditions of their own, that could be called nothing else but Acadian. Even their language was beginning to be a little different from the French spoken in France or in New Orleans.

Napoleon sold Louisiana to the United States in

1803. From then on, the Acadians were Americans in every legal way. Yet this made as little difference to them at first as had the change from Spanish to French ownership the year before. It must have been a long time before some of them even heard that they had become Americans.

Of course many of them did know of it. Some of them did not like it. These had hoped that Louisiana would remain French. In their memories and in those of their parents lingered the recollection of how some of them had been treated during the years they had lived in the English-speaking colonies. Yet they knew, too, that many of their men had helped the Americans and the Spanish to fight the British in the American Revolution. So most of them accepted this last change as not too bad.

When William C. C. Claiborne came to Louisiana as the first American governor, he made a study of the feelings of the Acadians about becoming Americans. He reported that among them Napoleon Bonaparte had many admirers who hoped that Louisiana would one day belong to France again. The American authorities thought, however, that the Acadians who felt this way were led to do so by owners of large plantations in or near the Acadian country.

These plantation owners were Creoles, most of them French, although some were Spanish, who hated the United States and feared American rule. They did not like this young republic or democracy. They thought it would deprive them of many of their privileges and of their wealth. The aristocrats who had remained in the neighborhood of St. Martinville felt that way, too. There were even attempts to stir up revolt against the American officials in New Orleans.

On the other hand, Pierre Clement de Laussat, who had been in charge of New Orleans for France while the Louisiana Purchase was taking place, had no hope Louisiana would ever be French again. He was grieved about this. He wrote that Americans would pour into Louisiana, and that it would become so American that everyone would be speaking English. He said it would grow and grow. Soon the Americans would make a great deal of money from its sugar and rice and cotton, and from using New Orleans as a port. Of course he was right.

Laussat wrote of the Acadians that they had "always distinguished themselves by their ardent love of France." He said they were "naturally gentle and docile, although touchy, proud and brave." However, he admitted, although he did not like the idea, that the Acadians would learn to like living under the government of the United States in the years to come. He was right about that, too.

In those days Louisiana had counties, and most of the Acadians lived in the counties of Acadia, Opelousas, Attakapas and Lafourche.

Claiborne himself visited some of these counties in 1805. Everywhere he found the Acadians becoming a prosperous people. They had great herds of cattle and their fields were rich with sugar, rice and corn. Some of the people who had arrived in New Orleans in dire poverty were already wealthy in cattle, land and crops. Their daily lives were simple, but pleasant. Few wanted for anything. And wherever Claiborne or his representatives went, they found the Acadians friendly. This was not always true of the aristocratic French and Spanish planters.

Yet although the Acadians were friendly, they were not ready to take an active part in American affairs or to fight on the side of the United States in war. A few years after Claiborne took office he had trouble with the Spanish authorities in the Floridas and in Texas. Claiborne called for volunteers for his militia. Few came from the Acadians. Many of them were actually sympathizers with the Spanish. The rest either knew nothing of these quarrels or cared little about them.

When American laws did touch them, the Acadians usually did not like that, either. They were used to living by their own rules. They were particularly opposed to trial by jury. That may seem strange to us, but they had never heard of it before and they did not like it. If one of their own people committed a crime they had always taken care of him in their own way. A court trial seemed to them a waste of time. They were too simple a people to understand it.

It was the Creoles of New Orleans, however, who gave Claiborne the most trouble. A proud and haughty people with fine manners, although few of them had much education at the time, they hated the Americans intensely. Claiborne did not understand them. They, in turn, rebelled against his entire administration. Everything he did offended them.

When Claiborne forbade the importation of more Negroes for slaves, the stubborn Creoles smuggled them in, a great many through Jean and Pierre Lafitte. These two men were famed smugglers and privateers, often called pirates, who did a huge business in smuggling from the islands and swamps where the Mississippi empties into the Gulf of Mexico. The Creoles, of course, were not alone in this. Many Americans bought slaves from the Lafitte brothers, too.

In 1810 a group of Acadians on Bayou Teche were accused of bringing slaves into the country. Then it was discovered that Acadians were not the smugglers at all. Instead, they were Americans, a rough crowd who had gone to live near the settlers from Nova Scotia. Later the same year a similar charge was made against the Acadians on Bayou Lafourche. Again they were proven innocent.

It is true that some Acadian youths did join Lafitte's band down at Barataria, but aside from that Acadians never were part of the slave traffic. So far as we know few of them ever owned slaves, including those who could, in time, afford it.

The Acadians are not to be condemned for not having wanted to mix with the Americans at this time. They wanted to live alone and in their own way. They wanted peace. They would not fight for a country they could not yet feel was really their own.

The year 1815 saw the Acadians for the first time taking a willing part in the defense of the United States. This was during the Battle of New Orleans when they fought beside Creoles from New Orleans, and men from Kentucky and Tennessee. Under General Jackson and Creole officers they were valiant soldiers.

Of course the fact that the British were the enemy may have played a part in their eagerness to help defend New Orleans on the plains of Chalmette below the city. They had felt the same way during the American Revolution. Yet, whatever the cause, their part in this great battle at the end of the War of 1812 brought them closer to the United States. It brought them closer to being Americans in the real sense of the word.

There were Acadian heroes in that struggle at the gates of New Orleans. Jackson and Claiborne did not forget. They honored them in the celebration that followed the victory.

Among those so honored was one elderly lady from St. Martinville, Madame Devince Bienvenue, always called Grandmère Devince. Her story has never been forgotten in Louisiana.

Grandmère Devince was not an Acadian herself, but the daughter of a French admiral. She had married an Acadian, and she had seven sons who were named Terville, Theodule, Terence, Timoleon, Timecourt, Casimir and Devince. All seven hurried to New Orleans and joined Andrew Jackson's forces in defending the city. Grandmère Devince sent a letter to Governor Claiborne along with them, too. In it she said that she was sorry she did not have more than seven sons to help save the city from the English, and she offered to come to New Orleans to help in the nursing of the wounded.

We don't know Grandmère's exact age at the time, but since her youngest son was nearly thirty years old, she must have been getting along in years. She had been brought up in San Domingo, and it is quite possible she remembered the arrival of Acadians there after they had been driven from Nova Scotia. It is probable, too, that her husband had been one of those exiles.

There is no record that Claiborne sent for her, but come she did. She arrived in New Orleans while the

Grandmère Devince was placed in a chair and was borne through the streets in the victory parade

battle raged, after what must have been a long, hard trip. She nursed the wounded and waited with the women of New Orleans for their men—and her own seven sons—to return from Chalmette in victory or in defeat.

When they marched home in triumph Grandmère was placed in a chair, which was set upon the shoulders of two soldiers, and was borne through the streets of the city in the victory parade. In one of the speeches during the celebration that followed, she was praised for her patriotism by General Jackson.

Thus the Battle of New Orleans was the beginning of the part Acadians were to play in American affairs.

17 *Through the Years*

HOWEVER, ALTHOUGH THEY BEGAN TO REALIZE THEY were citizens of the United States from that time on, no people in the country were slower to change than were the Acadians. They hated change. They resisted education. They refused to speak English.

Let alone, they were happy. When called upon for any kind of service to their new country, they served well and bravely. But then they returned to their own people.

Many of them continued to prosper. They pioneered in the production of rice. They had no help from outside. They preferred it that way. Their fields of sugar cane spread. Their cattle and sheep increased in number. Each year they offered more oysters and shrimp at the market places. The volume of fur pelts increased and in time became the largest in the nation.

As happens among all men and in all civilizations,

some grew much richer than others. Some remained very poor. But even the poor did not want for food or the bare necessities of life. Some worked harder than others. Some were luckier. But it was rare for an Acadian to take advantage of another, or to cheat another.

Their feeling of belonging to each other remained constant. It became a saying on the bayous that every man, rich or poor, was the next man's cousin. In time this became almost true, for their many children continued to intermarry with their neighbors' children.

The same names continued to be prominent among them. The old family names of Hebert, Leblanc, Mouton, Thibodeaux, Broussard, Landry and Bourgeois were well known in the Acadia of Nova Scotia. They continued to be well known in the Acadia of Louisiana. Today they are the names of the largest families of Acadian descent in the state. Probably each has at one time or another had a member who married into one or more of the other families. Thus they all feel that they are related.

Of course as they prospered they did improve their way of life. Better houses took the place of the shacks and the clay-and-stick cottages. A few families built fine Louisiana plantation houses, although they seldom

Acadian children began to learn to read and write

cared for elegance. Most of them continued to live simply. They were slow to adopt anything that was modern, or any of the new inventions that began to appear in other parts of the country.

When they began to build churches, they soon had their own priests. With the churches came schools in the settlements that began to form and which one day would be flourishing towns. The first schools were Catholic ones, for the Acadians did not like public schools for a long time.

Children began to learn to read and write for the first time in the histories of their families. In the towns some of these educated Acadians went into business, entered politics and the professions. Most of them, however, continued to live on and from the land as had their ancestors.

With the advent of education and prosperity some Acadians gave up their taste for complete isolation. The sons and daughters began to travel, at least as far as New Orleans. In time many began going there to school, to the opera, and on shopping expeditions. When the age of the steamboat arrived and these vessels plied the bayous, travel increased even more.

There began to be two kinds of Acadians: those who clung to their old ways and those who did not. Most of the people did not change. They lived as they had always lived. The women and girls dressed in the same style of clothing they had worn in Nova Scotia, wearing the wide skirts and crisp white aprons and the sunbonnet-like caps of their ancestors. They still could be found cooking at their outdoor kitchens, or working at their looms and spinning wheels. They still resisted education. They continued to refuse to learn English.

The others changed gradually. Usually these were people who lived in or near a town. It was they who went to school, who wore the fashions of the day, who even in time learned at least enough English to be understood.

The towns grew. With the invention of the steamboat came a period in which St. Martinville grew in importance both as a business town and as a summer resort to which many people from New Orleans went each year. The steamboat trip was just long enough to be pleasant, and St. Martinville became a stylish place to go. The residents prospered through this, and for a time it seemed that the village would become one of the most important towns in Louisiana.

But in 1855 it was visited by a terrible yellow fever epidemic. The same year a fire destroyed the entire business section. Shortly after that a hurricane almost wiped out the town. Then came the Civil War. After that the steamboats vanished from Bayou Teche, and when a railroad was built through that part of the state it did not go near St. Martinville. Today it is a charming, picturesque town, but no trace remains of the prosperity and business it once enjoyed.

While Claiborne was still governor the old counties were divided and from then on were called parishes. The counties that had been called Acadia, Attakapas, and Opelousas were split into smaller divisions and given new names. Later there were still other divisions. In these parishes, towns began to spring up.

For instance, a map made as early as 1816 shows the town of New Iberia on Bayou Teche. However, the town's incorporation did not actually take place until 1839. During steamboat days it was a busy shipping center, and today New Iberia is called "The Queen City of the Teche." It is the home of great salt mines, of seafood and vegetable canneries, of the oil industry, of tabasco sauce, and of many kinds of business. In all these, thousands of the Acadians' descendants are employed.

The history of the town of Lafayette is even more directly connected with the Acadians. Now it is the seat of what is called Lafayette Parish, but it was once part of old Attakapas County. It had its start as a plantation settlement established by Andrew Martin and two brothers named Jean and Marin Mouton, who were the ancestors of one of the most prominent Acadian families in Louisiana.

Salvator and Anne Mouton, the parents of the Mouton brothers, had been exiled from Nova Scotia by the British, taking with them young Jean. It is said that

Salvator and Anne, together with Jean, who was still a small child, had hidden out in the woods and lived on berries for ten days. They reached New Orleans in 1765 with the first group of Acadians. There Marin was born.

Jean and Marin Mouton, with Andrew Martin, were living where Lafayette is now situated as early as the late 1770s. In 1824 Jean laid out the settlement and called it Vermillionville. By 1842 the town had a bank, schools, and a newspaper which was printed in both French and English. In 1884 its name was changed to Lafayette.

Lafayette remains very French, very Acadian. French is spoken by most of its residents, although nearly all of them now speak English, too. Dudley J. LeBlanc organized the Louisiana Association of Acadians there in 1930. In 1930 and 1936 this association sponsored pilgrimages to Nova Scotia, during which the women and girls making the trips wore Acadian costumes. In 1931 and in 1940 Nova Scotia Acadians visited Lafayette and other places along the Bayou Teche. In later years, Louisiana Acadians have made other pilgrimages to Nova Scotia.

Acadians founded many other Louisiana towns. Houma, named after the Houma tribe of Indians, spreads over a tract of land that once belonged to Joseph Hache, an exile from Nova Scotia who settled there in 1800. Thibodaux was the first trading center established between New Orleans and the Teche country. It was named after a governor of Louisiana, Henry Schuyler Thibodaux, who was himself partly of Acadian descent. There are numerous small towns and centers that bear Acadian names, such as Broussard, Labadieville, and Chauvin.

Of course all this progress was often interrupted by war. The Acadians sent their young men to fight in the Mexican War, and again in the Civil War. In later wars, such as World War I and World War II, they have, naturally, played as important a part as any other group of Americans.

Yet the Acadians still remain a distinct people in many ways. As has been said before, not all Acadian families remained pure French in blood. They have been in Louisiana for nearly two hundred years, and during that time they have intermarried with almost every other nationality.

They still have great affection for one another and

much pride in their ancestry. Those among them who have remained simple in their ways of life have many interesting and curious customs. It is a way of life unlike any other in the world.

18 *Softshell Crabs and the Loup-Garou*

"A CAJUN IS HIS OWN MAN. HE DON'T LIKE TO WORK for nobody else, no! You see a Cajun? You see a free man. He got him a boat, his house, his traps. He catch the shrimp. He take care of hisself and his family. That's the way it's always been. You see a Cajun, you looking at a man who stands on his own two feets his whole, entire life!"

That is old Gaston Boudreaux talking. Gaston calls himself a "Cajun" because that is Louisiana slang for Acadians. They often call themselves that, and they do not mind when other people do. In a way it has become a term of affection.

Gaston has always lived the typical, simple life of his kind of Acadian. There are thousands like him all over Louisiana. In the winter he is a fur trapper, catching the muskrat. During other times of the year he takes his big nets and goes out in his boats searching for shrimp. He has taken jobs a few times during his life, but only when he had to, and he was never happy in them.

He can speak English when he has to do so, but he doesn't like it. He speaks French at home and among his friends. He has little education, but he can sign his name and he can strike a shrewd bargain with his pelts and shrimp. All his children have gone to school, however, and he has one granddaughter at the Louisiana State University in Baton Rouge, Louisiana, of whom he is extremely proud. "She's got plenty of brains in her head, her," he'll tell you.

Gaston's English is typically Cajun. Cajun English is different from any other. For one thing, all Acadians have a tremendous sense of humor. For another, their English is an almost exact translation of their French. They use double negatives constantly. Sometimes they even use three negatives, and then attach a "no" at the end of the sentence. For instance, a Cajun might say, "He wouldn't do nothing I asked him not to do, no!" Many sentences end in pronouns: "She come by my house two times last week to see me, her."

Pronouns always fly freely. Young people meeting along the bayou will greet each other by saying, "What you know, you?" They will ask, "How your mama, her?" Inanimate objects are also discussed by the use of personal pronouns: "How your roof, Joe? She hold up in that storm, yes? She look weak to me."

The typical Cajun is nervous, sensitive and impatient. He talks with his eyes, his hands, his shoulders, almost as much as with his tongue. Emphasis is often strong in all declarations, no matter whether they are affirmative or negative: "I'm gonna get me a new boat next fall, yes! She gonna be so pretty the shrimps gonna jump right in, you'll see!"

Exaggerations are the rule, not the exception. Listen to Etienne telling his friend, Aristide, about the charivari given him at his wedding. (At a Cajun charivari all the friends of the bride and groom gather outside the house where the wedding is being celebrated and beat on pots and pans, blow horns and ring cowbells, and in every way make as much noise as possible.) But Etienne was not content with describing his charivari as having been of that normally noisy variety. He had to tell Aristide, who was away on a trip at the time, "They make so much noise for me, the moon she fall out of the sky and go in the bayou. Like boom!"

Emphasis is always strong in regard to personal pride

in a Cajun's property, and in everything he does. A Cajun will tell you he is the best fisherman "in the whole, entire world, me!" A Cajun girl is not always without pride in her beauty. Tell one she is pretty and she is likely to reply, "You is tell me something what I already know!"

And Acadian French is not the French taught in schools today, either here or in France. A visitor from Paris might have a hard time understanding some of it. It is a mixture of a kind of French spoken centuries ago, words borrowed from Spanish, English, Indian and Negro dialects, and words of the Acadians' own invention.

Many of these invented words are amusing, and the whole language is sprinkled with humorous phrases. For instance, if a Cajun wants to tell you a man is hard-boiled or tough, he is likely to say the man is a softshell crab. At a dance you are likely to find a room called *le parc des petits,* which means, almost literally, "park the babies." It is the room where parents leave the babies to sleep while they dance.

Of a girl or woman who dresses herself up, curls her hair and uses makeup, and is also known as a flirt, a Cajun will say, "Her, she is all *frisée* and *rougie*. Every time she sees a young man she roll her eyes, *toute gougou*!" Of a happily married couple Cajuns will always say, "They are like *deux colombes*!" Like two doves. Of a couple who quarrel they will say that they are "Like two crabs in a net!" A Cajun parent will tell a child who gets low marks at school, "You is *bête comme un chou*," although no one seems to know why the young boy or girl should be compared with a cabbage.

They have many proverbs and these are often amusing. To a person who talks too much they will say, *"On lave son linge sale en famille!"* That is, "Wash your clothes in your family." Of someone who is bright they will say, "His brains is sewed with white thread."

When it is raining Cajuns are likely to say, *"Çà grimace,"* which means it (the sky) is frowning, or making a face. Of an automobile wreck they will say it was *"un naufrage,"* which means a shipwreck, but has come to mean any other kind as well. They will also sometimes say, *"Je vais naviguer"*—"I am going to navigate." Then they simply mean they are going out. For "vamose" (a Spanish word meaning "get out") they often say "bamose."

A person who is thought giddy is frequently called a

frou-frou. And "clown" is probably used more often in the bayou country than any other place in the world. Names of animals and other creatures are also applied to people for various reasons. A man who stays out late at night may be called a bullfrog. He croaks in the swamps all night, they will tell you to explain their meaning. Many Cajuns even describe their homes in ways that may sound odd to some of us, calling them *îles*—islands—because the home is set in a wooded grove in the prairie country. Whole villages have come by their names in other peculiar ways. For instance, one called Pin Hook received that name because of an early settler who used to steal his neighbors' chickens by attaching a bent pin to a long string and a piece of corn, and thus coaxing the chickens out of a neighbor's yard. General Dick Taylor fought a Civil War battle at Pin Hook, Louisiana.

Cajun English has of course even come to life on signs. At various places along the highways and roads you can today see such signs as "Stop and eat, we fix you up!" or "Pants pressed while you hide," and "Car wash and shine for you quick."

Cajuns love all kinds of fun, especially dancing. Saturday-night dances are popular everywhere in the

Acadian country. These used to be called *fais dodos,* but that term, which meant "go to sleep," is seldom heard any longer. (No one except the babies in *le parc des petits* ever went to sleep at a *fais dodo,* for Saturday-night dances often go on until early in the morning.) The music used to come from local talent, with a fiddler, a guitarist and a piano player performing, and you may still find some of that kind in more remote sections. Nowadays, however, juke boxes and phonographs are more common. Acadian children all dance, as well as older people, and everybody has a good time. A Cajun will say he "passed a good time." That is one of his favorite expressions.

They love sports, too. Pirogue races have long been popular. The pirogues used today are exactly the same kind of boats the early Acadians used to hollow from single logs. Now there is an annual pirogue race on Bayou Barataria. Trappers and fishermen from all over Louisiana take part, and many visitors from towns and cities come to watch it. The boats move with amazing speed and the races are exciting contests.

Frog hunts are popular as a nighttime sport, young boys taking as much part as their fathers. Crawfishing is an important industry, but people do it for fun, too. There is even a little song about it:

Poor crawfish ain't got no show
Frenchmen catch 'em and make gumbo.

In the prairie country young Acadians are skillful and daring horsemen. Usually they ride small horses called "Creole ponies." These are descendants of the wild mustangs which the first Acadians in Louisiana caught and tamed. They are fiery little animals, full of life and "pep." Young men love to train them to prance and dance and perform all kinds of tricks.

Of course all the sports enjoyed by Americans in other parts of the country are popular, too. Most Acadians are excellent swimmers. And far back in the bayous and swamps boys and men play baseball and football, and follow national leagues and games, for radio and television have penetrated almost everywhere.

Hunting and fishing are sports as well as ways of earning a living. The duck season is a busy time on the bayous. Fishing goes on all year long. Shrimping is big business, of course. There are more than fifty thousand

Once a year there are blessings of the shrimp fleets

Cajuns employed in the shrimp industry. Boats go out as far as forty miles in the Gulf of Mexico.

Once a year there are blessings of the shrimp fleets. In August the Roman Catholic Archbishop, accompanied by bishops, priests and other attendants, goes from New Orleans into the Acadian country to bless the boats and the men who are engaged in catching shrimp. There are masses and elaborate ceremonies. All the boats and trawlers are decorated with flags and pennants, and thousands of Cajuns come to take part in the celebration. Everybody wears his Sunday clothes. People bring food. The celebration is half religious, half a picnic. Everybody "passes a good time."

Cajuns love to eat. They are among the best cooks in the world. They love gumbos—thick soups made of crabs, shrimp, oysters, and ham. They also make a chicken gumbo, which is one of the best things to eat in the world, and another gumbo with hot sausages. They love jambalaya, a combination of rice, tomatoes, and any kind of seafood and meat. They love frog legs, and crawfish bisque—which, like gumbo, is a kind of soup. They cook oysters in fifty different ways. They feast on the hardshell crab and also on the softshell crab, when it is in season.

Coffee is a drink they pour down their throats all day long. They make their coffee as black as ink and as strong as possible, and they drink it with lots of sugar. They seldom use cream, although many use hot milk. The coffee pot is never empty on any Cajun's stove.

Like their ancestors, most of them marry at a young age and have many children. They give their children curious and amusing names at times. Greek names are popular. There are hundreds of boys named Achille and Ulysse along the bayous. Some families like to name all their children with given names starting with the same letter. One family chose the letter "O" and the children were named Odile, Odelia, Odalia, Olive, Oliver, Olivia, Ophelia, Odelin, Octave, Octavia, Ovide, Onesia, Olita, Otta, Omea and Opta. However, this makes little difference, for few Cajun children —or grownups either—are ever called by their real names. Everybody has a nickname, and sometimes the real name is almost forgotten.

Also, certain nicknames are popular, and many people in entirely different families will have the same one. It is said that every Cajun family, for instance, has someone in it called "Coon." Almost all have a Toots, a Boots, a Noo-noo, a Ti-ti, a Lala, a Mannie, a Bos and a Bébé. They carry these nicknames all their lives. An old lady of eighty-eight may be called Tante Bébé—Aunt Baby—all her days. Once she was the baby of her family and so was called Bébé. Then she became Tante Bébé to her nieces and nephews, and to everyone else who knew her.

Like their ancestors, the Cajuns of today are very devoted to their families. They help one another in time of trouble much more than do most people nowadays. They will take in any of their relatives and support them if they must, and will do it cheerfully. It is almost unknown for an Acadian child to be put out for adoption or to be sent to an orphanage should his parents die. There is almost always an aunt or uncle to take the homeless child, or, if not, a neighbor will.

Old people are cared for, too. They do not go to old folks' homes. Someone will always take in the old aunt or grandmother—the *tante* or *mère*—and she will be welcome. It would be thought disgraceful to do anything else. It would be disgraceful, too, to make old people think they are a burden. It is a pleasure to have *tante* or *mère*. The more relatives Acadians have in their homes the happier they seem to be.

There are many superstitions on the bayous, but few

of them are taken seriously now. Most of them are jokes. They are a part of Cajun humor, although strangers may be told of them with serious faces, in hope that they will be believed.

There is still the *loup-garou.* He is fading slowly these days and may soon be forgotten, but stories about him are still told in some places.

The *loups-garous* are werewolves—people who can change themselves into wolves at night, usually on nights when the moon is full. Then they may attack people and bite them, and the bitten persons will become *loups-garous,* too. It is said *loups-garous* ride bats as big as airplanes. *Loups-garous* hold dances and balls, usually at a place called Bayou Goula. There they dance together all night long and have a lot of fun.

There are said to be only two ways to kill or capture a *loup-garou.* It can't be shot. Bullets go right through it. But if you throw a frog at one he will run away, because *loups-garous* are supposed to be afraid of frogs. The other way to fight one is to hang a big shrimp net from a tree. Then a *loup-garou* will get himself caught in it, and you can sprinkle him with salt. The salt will make him shrink until he disappears. Of course no one has ever caught a *loup-garou*. No one has ever really seen one.

Another imaginary creature is the *letiche*. He is the ghost of a baby who died without being baptized. He is supposed to wander around at night trying to find children to play with him. Of course no one has ever seen him, either. Nobody believes in him. There are many other such stories—about mermaids in the bayous, and appearances of devils—but it is all in fun.

There are many Cajun customs that are different from those of most other Americans. There are many religious holidays that are celebrated in various ways. Perhaps the most curious custom of all, however, is the way and the time that some Cajun trappers celebrate Christmas.

Of course we all know Christmas comes on December 25th. This is in the middle of the trapping season. So the trappers do not celebrate it then at all. Families are so busy at this time that even school sessions may be changed in places where most people make their living from trapping. Schools run all summer, then close in the fall.

Long before Christmas entire families leave home and travel into the swamps and woods to the cabins in which they live most of the winter. Children often help their fathers set the traps and skin the animals that are caught. Furs and skins must be treated. When the season is over in the early spring the whole family returns home, its boats loaded with furs to be sold for money which will support them all the rest of the year. Some trappers make lots of money.

Then Christmas can be celebrated, usually in February or March, and the Cajuns enjoy it as much as if it came at the regular time. Churches hold Christmas services. Houses are decorated just as they would have been for December 25th. Christmas trees are lighted, Santa Claus arrives, and presents are distributed. Then the children go back to school.

It may seem strange to us, but people can make any changes that are necessary to fit their way of life.

19 *The Real Evangeline*

SOUTHWESTERN LOUISIANA REALLY BELONGS TO THE Acadian. It is his land, his new Acadia, in every sense of these words. Thousands of people of other races and backgrounds live there. They own land and the Acadian may even live on land owned by these other people. They have great industries and businesses, and the Acadian may work for them. Yet this is the Acadian's country. He has put his own mark upon everything—upon the customs, the traditions, the history, even the food and the language.

This is the Cajun's world, and everyone knows it. He has won his place in many ways, not the least important of them being his kindness, his gentleness, his hospitality and generosity.

Rich or poor, educated or unable to read and write, in many ways all Acadians are the same. Drive along any highway by automobile, walk any road beside the

Buggies drawn by horses are still in constant use

bayous, or penetrate the deep swamps by boat, and if you stop at any Acadian home you will find your welcome much the same. The coffee pot will always be hot. Everyone will seem glad to see you. Even the dogs and cats and chickens will have a happy look.

In some localities in this part of Louisiana newspapers are still printed in two languages, English and French. Old customs are kept up. The Acadian country is one of the few places in the United States where buggies, drawn by horses, are still in constant use. This is true especially around Abbéville, an Acadian town. Here buggies are still being manufactured and sold. More than half the buggies now being made in the United States come from there.

Buggies can still be seen around Lafayette, although it is a modern town of good size. Here, as in many places, the Acadian custom of serving coffee at three o'clock in the afternoon, an hour when friends visit, is kept by nearly everyone in town. Not far from Lafayette people can still be found who speak no English, but only Acadian French.

All along Bayou Lafourche the Acadians are the largest part of the population. Bayou Lafourche has been called "the longest street in the United States." For eighty-five miles towns and villages and houses line its banks. It ends near the Gulf of Mexico, and in this section there are many families who have never learned to speak English and who live almost as did their great-great-grandfathers. However, more and more young people are beginning to speak the language of the rest of the United States.

On Bayou Petit Caillou (little pebble) some families still live in huts with thatched roofs, usually made of the wild palmetto. Cooking is done in the open air. Trappers and shrimpers, the men still carve out their own pirogues, make their own huge nets. Most families raise vegetables and some a little sugar cane. The women work outdoors in some places; they fish and make mattresses of Spanish moss, gathered from the live oak and other trees. Children work with their parents in the old Acadian fashion, although all young people also go to school nowadays. They are forced to do so by law.

The Acadians build few monuments to their past. But at old St. Martinville the grave of Evangeline is shown to visitors. This is not the same Evangeline who appears in Longfellow's poem, although the Acadians will tell you the two girls were identical.

According to the story, the young woman who is buried at St. Martinville was named Emmeline Labiche. Like Evangeline in the poem, she was separated from her sweetheart when they were both exiled from Nova Scotia. His real name was not Gabriel, but Louis Arceneaux.

Emmeline suffered just as did Evangeline. She wandered for a long time, trying to find Louis. Like Evangeline in her search for Gabriel, Emmeline almost found him several times, but always just barely missed him.

At last Emmeline came to St. Martinville, traveling

down beautiful Bayou Teche in a frail pirogue. When she set foot on the earth there, under a spreading live oak, she met Louis Arceneaux. And here the story changes from the one Longfellow wrote about Evangeline.

Longfellow's Evangeline did not find Gabriel until much later. When this happened, he was dying in Philadelphia, and she, after years of waiting, had become a nun.

The tragedy of Emmeline Labiche is different. At the time of her meeting with Louis Arceneaux he was about to be married to another girl and had almost forgotten Emmeline. Some versions say he thought she was dead. Anyway, he was in love with someone else.

According to this Acadian story, Emmeline then went insane. She died a little while after that, and was buried near the church in St. Martinville. Now there is a statue over her grave. It was posed for by Dolores Del Rio, a motion-picture actress who starred in a moving picture of *Evangeline* about twenty years ago. Later, Miss Del Rio donated the statue to the town. Today it is called the Evangeline Monument.

We do not know if Emmeline Labiche and Louis Arceneaux were the same people as Longfellow's Evangeline and Gabriel. Yet it is possible, perhaps even likely. It could easily have been Emmeline's story that Longfellow heard from Nathaniel Hawthorne and his friends. Why not? There may have been many Evangelines and Gabriels.

The oak under which Emmeline Labiche landed still stands on the banks of the bayou, too. It is a gigantic old tree with immense spreading limbs. Cement benches have been placed beneath it, and visitors sit there and try to picture in their minds the landing of Evangeline (or Emmeline) at this beautiful spot almost two hundred years ago.

Evangeline is remembered in many ways in the St. Martinville section of the state. The parish in which the town is located is now called St. Martin Parish. And near by is the Longfellow-Evangeline Memorial Park, which was established as a state park in 1934. In the center of the park is an old Acadian cottage. It is said that the cottage of Louis Arceneaux once stood near it. The house now standing is used as a museum. It contains all kinds of written records and relics left by the early Acadians. They have not been forgotten.

20 *The Acadians Today*

MORE THAN A HALF MILLION DESCENDANTS OF THE original Acadian exiles live in Louisiana today. Of course not all are fishermen, trappers or farmers. Not all are country folk. Not by far. The Acadian of today may follow any occupation or profession. Many men and women of Acadian descent are among the most highly educated and cultured people in the state. Many are prosperous. Many live and work in the towns and cities and have done so for some generations.

There have been Acadian governors of Louisiana. There have been Acadian senators and congressmen. There are Acadians in all branches of politics. There are Acadian doctors, lawyers, teachers, writers, poets, painters, and all kinds of businessmen. Acadians have grown rich in sugar, rice, oil, and other industries. They keep shops and stores, run factories and restaurants, and do all the other things men do everywhere in America to earn their livings. In these ways they are as different as are people anywhere else. They remain alike in that they all feel they are kin, that they are of one people. Of that they are proud.

Education was a little late in reaching the bayous, but it has spread swiftly during the past twenty-five years or so, and it is still spreading. Practically all children receive some schooling now, even in the most remote parts of the country. In the towns most of them go to high school and many go to college.

Until 1917, when the United States entered World War I, there were thousands of Acadians in the swamps and along the bayous who had no interest in learning to speak English. These were the shrimpers, fishermen and trappers who seldom saw anybody but each other and rarely met an English-speaking person. Then the young men went into the army, learned English and took it back home.

After that, highways began cutting into all sections of the state, and the automobile brought thousands of visitors and tourists. Few Cajuns were cut off from the rest of the world any longer. Movies, radios and television sets have done the rest. They must know English to enjoy these amusements. In World War II Acadian men traveled far again.

It is still possible, of course, to find persons who don't speak English. Most of these live far, far from what we call civilization. Others are old people who can't learn it at their age, or simply refuse to do so. But this condition is fading fast. Now even most of the simplest Cajuns speak it, although with an accent.

Educated Acadians are intensely interested in their own people and the history of their ancestors. They continue to preserve many of their traditions and customs. Besides the pilgrimages they have made to Nova Scotia to visit the few Acadian descendants living there today, they hold festivals and take part in other events completely their own. On these occasions they dress in the costumes of long ago and revive some of the old customs.

Every year there are crop festivals throughout southwest Louisiana, such as the Sugar Cane Festival, the Shrimp Festival, the Rice Festival, the Orange Festival, and many others. Mardi Gras, or Shrove Tuesday, is celebrated in many towns throughout the section. In all these events Acadians play a large part, although everyone else does, too.

Acadian humor is heard everywhere. There are thousands of Acadian jokes, which all of them like to tell, and many sayings that all of them continue to use. Even the most highly educated Acadian may like to use an Acadian (or Cajun) accent. He may use it all the time or he may use it only when it pleases him to do so. Everyone in the bayou country loves to repeat sayings Cajuns are supposed to have said, such as: "You see ma cow down by de bayou, you push him home, heh? He been gone tree day now—yesterday, today and tomorrow!"

Of course Acadians travel everywhere now, and not only when they go to war. Yet most seem to prefer to remain at home. Probably fewer have left their home towns, their farms or their own people to live permanently in another part of the country than has any other group in America.

They have achieved a strong blending of the old and the new insofar as their towns are concerned. These towns are modern. There is everything in them that is to be found in any town anywhere in the United States. There are modern business sections, handsome buildings and streets, bus lines, lovely homes, fine schools and stores.

Yet the towns are different. A bayou edges nearly every one. The streets are usually shaded by the old live oak trees. In the restaurants, as well as in the private homes of the people who live there, the favorite dishes are Acadian ones—gumbo and jambalaya, crawfish

The Acadians give big "boils" in their back yards

bisque and softshell crabs. Everyone dances on Saturday nights and goes to church on Sunday mornings.

Everybody loves to hunt and fish, and in season entire families, including children and often grandparents, go crabbing and shrimping and crawfishing. They bring their catch home by the bucketful, share it with neighbors, and give big "boils" in their back yards.

At these parties the seafood, boiled beforehand with various seasonings, is passed around iced and on platters. An Acadian can eat more crabs and shrimp and crawfish than anyone on earth can eat of anything else.

Publicity has come to the Acadians, too. Now the world knows at least a little about them. There have been books and articles written about them, and there have been moving pictures and popular songs, such as "Shrimp Boats" and "Jambalaya."

This is a beautiful part of the United States, where live a warm, good and friendly people. Here these descendants of the Acadian exiles have found happiness. Perhaps it is a reward for the bravery and the faith of their ancestors. In any case, it seems to the Acadians of today that John Smith, the founder of the colony of Virginia, might well have been speaking of Louisiana when he said of the whole continent:

"Heaven and earth never agreed better to frame a place for Man's habitation!"

Index

Index

LANDMARK BOOKS

1 The Voyages of Christopher Columbus
2 The Landing of the Pilgrims
3 Pocahontas and Captain John Smith
4 Paul Revere and the Minute Men
5 Our Independence and the Constitution
6 The California Gold Rush
7 The Pony Express
8 Lee and Grant at Appomattox
9 The Building of the First Transcontinental Railroad
10 The Wright Brothers
11 Prehistoric America
12 The Vikings
13 The Santa Fe Trail
14 The Story of the U.S. Marines
15 The Lewis and Clark Expedition
16 The Monitor and the Merrimac
17 The Explorations of Pere Marquette
18 The Panama Canal
19 The Pirate LaFitte and the Battle of New Orleans
20 Custer's Last Stand
21 Daniel Boone
22 Clipper Ship Days
23 Gettysburg
24 The Louisiana Purchase
25 Wild Bill Hickock Tames the West
26 Betsy Ross and the Flag
27 The Conquest of the North and South Poles
28 Ben Franklin of Old Philadelphia
29 Trappers and Traders of the Far West
30 Mr. Bell Invents the Telephone
31 The Barbary Pirates
32 Sam Houston, the Tallest Texan
33 The Winter at Valley Forge
34 The Erie Canal
35 Thirty Seconds Over Tokyo
36 Thomas Jefferson, Father of Democracy
37 The Coming of the Mormons
38 George Washington Carver
39 John Paul Jones, Fighting Sailor
40 The First Overland Mail
41 Teddy Roosevelt and the Rough Riders
42 To California by Covered Wagon
43 Peter Stuyvesant of Old New York
44 Lincoln and Douglas: The Years of Decision
45 Robert Fulton and the Steamboat
46 The F.B.I.
47 Dolly Madison
48 John James Audubon
49 Hawaii, Gem of the Pacific
50 War Chief of the Seminoles
51 Old Ironsides: The Fighting *Constitution*
52 The Mississippi Bubble
53 Kit Carson and the Wild Frontier
54 Robert E. Lee and the Road of Honor
55 Guadalcanal Diary
56 Commodore Perry and the Opening of Japan
57 Davy Crockett
58 Clara Barton, Founder of the American Red Cross
59 The Story of San Francisco
60 Up the Trail from Texas
61 Abe Lincoln: Log Cabin to White House
62 The Story of D-Day: June 6, 1944
63 Rogers' Rangers and the French and Indian War
64 The World's Greatest Showman: The Life of P. T. Barnum
65 Sequoyah: Leader of the Cherokees
66 Ethan Allen and the Green Mountain Boys
67 Wyatt Earp: U.S. Marshal
68 The Early Days of Automobiles
69 The Witchcraft of Salem Village
70 The West Point Story
71 George Washington: Frontier Colonel
72 The Texas Rangers

73 Buffalo Bill's Great Wild West Show
74 Evangeline and the Acadians
75 The Story of the Secret Service
76 Tippecanoe and Tyler Too!
77 America's First World War: General Pershing and the Yanks
78 The Doctors Who Conquered Yellow Fever
79 Remember the Alamo!
80 Andrew Carnegie and the Age of Steel
81 Geronimo: Wolf of the Warpath
82 The Story of the Paratroops
83 The American Revolution
84 The Story of the Naval Academy
85 Alexander Hamilton and Aaron Burr
86 Stonewall Jackson
87 The Battle for the Atlantic
88 The First Transatlantic Cable
89 The Story of the U.S. Air Force
90 The Swamp Fox of the Revolution
91 Heroines of the Early West
92 The Alaska Gold Rush
93 The Golden Age of Railroads
94 From Pearl Harbor to Okinawa

WORLD LANDMARK BOOKS

W-1 The First Men in the World
W-2 Alexander the Great
W-3 Adventures and Discoveries of Marco Polo
W-4 Joan of Arc
W-5 King Arthur and His Knights
W-6 Mary, Queen of Scots
W-7 Napoleon and the Battle of Waterloo
W-8 Royal Canadian Mounted Police
W-9 The Man Who Changed China: The Story of Sun Yat-Sen
W-10 The Battle of Britain
W-11 The Crusades
W-12 Genghis Khan and the Mongol Horde
W-13 Queen Elizabeth and the Spanish Armada
W-14 Simon Bolivar, the Great Liberator
W-15 The Slave Who Freed Haiti: The Story of Toussaint Louverture
W-16 The Story of Scotland Yard
W-17 The Life of St. Patrick
W-18 The Exploits of Xenophon
W-19 Captain Cook Explores the South Seas
W-20 Marie Antoinette
W-21 Will Shakespeare and the Globe Theater
W-22 The French Foreign Legion
W-23 Martin Luther
W-24 The Hudson's Bay Company
W-25 Balboa: Swordsman and Conquistador
W-26 The Magna Charta
W-27 Leonardo Da Vinci
W-28 General Brock and Niagara Falls
W-29 Catherine the Great
W-30 The Fall of Constantinople
W-31 Ferdinand Magellan: Master Mariner
W-32 Garibaldi: Father of Modern Italy
W-33 The Story of Albert Schweitzer
W-34 The Marquis de Lafayette: Bright Sword for Freedom
W-35 Famous Pirates of the New World
W-36 Exploring the Himalaya
W-37 Queen Victoria
W-38 The Flight and Adventures of Charles II
W-39 Chief of the Cossacks
W-40 The Adventures of Ulysses
W-41 William the Conqueror
W-42 Jesus of Nazareth
W-43 Julius Caesar
W-44 The Story of Australia
W-45 Captain Cortés Conquers Mexico
W-46 Florence Nightingale

Landmark
BOOKS